SHERMAN in CHERAW
and the Aftermath

By
ADELINE GODFREY MERRILL

First Printing 2009
2nd Printing and Revised by Adeline Godfrey Merrill

Copyright 2014 Adeline Godfrey Merrill

ISBN: 0615989802
ISBN 13: 9780615989808
Library of Congress Control Number: 2014905527
Margaret Pringle Latshaw, Parkville, MO

To Mother and Daddy

with eternal gratitude
for the wonderful experience of
growing up in Cheraw

ACKNOWLEDGEMENTS

The realization of this endeavor would not have been possible without the valuable assistance of many individuals. Several, however, have been constant and helpful throughout and they deserve special attention.

Peyre and Mary Pringle - for typing and transcribing into the computer my manuscript (which had been typed on an old IBM typewriter). This took time and patience. And I thank them for their editing talents also. They completed the first section of this book.

Mark and Margaret Pringle Latshaw - for undertaking the project of having this book published, as a gift to me. What an incredibly loving gesture!

Laurence L. Prince (deceased) - for giving me his family *Memoirs* about Sherman in Cheraw. The two accounts of his grandfather and of his great-aunt are the main nucleus of this story.

To my daughter "Sis" (Adeline B. Merrill) - for giving me the idea of writing about the strong women who faced Sherman's troops. This is what propelled the book into existence. She was particularly interested in looking at it from a woman's perspective.

Sources

- I leaned heavily on two authors, Larry E. Nelson and Burke Davis: *Sherman's March Through the Upper Pee Dee Region of South Carolina by* Larry E. Nelson and *Sherman's March by* Burke Davis. These books helped me fill in the gaps of understanding as to what happened before the Union troops arrived in Cheraw. Without their facts, I could not have told this story.

- Jacqueline Glass Campbell, author of the article in *Historical Society Magazine*, "When Sherman Marched North from the Sea: Resistance on the Confederate Home Front."

- Margaret P. Kinny's article on Pegues House.

- Ada Evans Stevenson (deceased), who provided me with photographs of the 10th of May ceremonies, various old houses, and letters from her grandfather (written while a prisoner of War at Johnson Island).

- "Sis" Huntley Hoover (deceased), for UDC Confederate papers and information about the first Confederate Monument.

Photographs:
Marshall & Susan McMillan - pictures of old covered bridge
Peyre G. Pringle - family portraits and houses
Sarah & Jim Spruill - photos of The Teacherage

- George Premmel and Mr. Henry Boyd, for new material about the Merchants Bank's role regarding Confederate Treasury Dept.

- *Old Cheraw Chronicle* articles were my main source.

INTRODUCTION

Let me explain that as a pre-teenager I had a passion for collecting articles, photographs, and histories of the old houses in Cheraw. These I obtained from the *Cheraw Chronicle*, but alas, I failed to put the dates on these articles. Therefore the dates I added are approximate guesses (between 1930-1935).

I have used primary sources (family letters, diaries, and other writings) to let the voices from the past take part in the telling of this story. It reveals the feelings of the Southerners, which existed for several generations. I am happy that these feeling are at long last behind us. But I realize that as far as this latest generation is concerned, that story of the Lost Cause Movement seems to have been forgotten. That is the purpose of this little book.

As I quote these various family records, occasionally some remarks are put in italics. That means that I am the speaker. Those words are mine.

Adeline Godfrey Merrill
Nov. 2009

SHERMAN IN CHERAW

INTRODUCTION

Quote from an article in *The South Carolina Historical Society Magazine*, July 2006, Volume 107 #3 by Jacqueline Glass Campbell. (She is the author of *When Sherman Marched North from the Sea: Resistance on the Confederate Home Front*).

Author Jacqueline Campbell contributes fresh, thought-provoking insights into a long neglected area of study – the interaction between General Sherman's soldiers and southern civilians, black and white, male and female, during his march through the Carolinas. "Sherman's advance northward from Savannah, undertaken to demoralize the South and to destroy its will to continue the war, raises questions regarding racial attitudes, gender ideology, and perceptions of the military as a cultural entity. It is an effort to separate long cherished myth from reality."

    Quote from author Frank Burroughs, a cousin who stopped by to see me while in Charleston. I was not at home, so he wrote this little note; "Here I am in Charleston with its long, eventful and emphatically unforgotten past." What I want to do is tell a part of our state's history which is, for all practical purposes, an emphatically <u>forgotten past.</u>

Campbell focuses on the less documented march through South and North Carolina, where home front and battlefront merged in early 1865. "That march becomes a more complex story. It illuminated the importance of culture for determining the limits of war and how it is fought. If we understand war as culturally sanctioned violence, we can place a military campaign in a much broader social context."

"After capturing Savannah, which surrendered without a fight, Sherman noted that civilians accepted Federal occupation with a minimum of struggle, and that while many cold and hungry people welcomed the arrival of Federal troops and the distribution of supplies, others hid burning resentment and sought to survive through enterprise and manipulation."

Campbell presents the hypothesis that while civilians may have appeared despondent at their first experience of captivity, this response could have been the initial phase of rededication to the Southern Cause.

"When Sherman invaded South Carolina he invaded a land protected by females. Society's concept of Womanhood at that time encompassed a definitive gender attitude: that is, women should be pious, reverent, dependent, family oriented, and above all, obedient. Confederate women broke the culturally imposed shackles of restraints, and bravely defended their homes and families with fierce determination of defiance, shocking northern soldiers with their refusal to accept defeat."

"Federal soldiers accused Confederate women of perpetuating the war by not cowing and cooperating with them. While resisting Sherman on the home front, South Carolina women urged their men to remain at their posts. Thus, a secondary battlefront came to exist between Federal soldiers and Confederate females. Women were willing to fight for their rights and defend their homes."

Campbell was perplexed with yet another vexing question: Why has the myth of their passivity existed so long? Why the diametrically opposed mid-nineteenth century concept of passive womanhood versus the great strength displayed when forced to face an invading enemy?

Quote from *All in One Southern Family, Volume II, Life in Cheraw*
by Adeline G. Merrill

THE TENTH OF MAY

Mary Chestnut:
"The camp songs of these men were a heartbreak—so sad, yet so stirring. They would have warmed the blood of an Icelander. The leading voice was powerful, mellow, clear, distinct, pathetic, sweet---so I sat down as women have done before when they hung up their harps by strange streams, and I wept."
(Allusion to Psalm 137)

From Ad:
It is hard for my children to fathom the fact that my lifespan reaches back to a time when I can remember Confederate War veterans leading parades—as we marched to the cemetery on the tenth of May.

The Tenth of May Ceremonies, Cheraw, South Carolina

This was the date of the death of General Stonewall Jackson. South Carolina and North Carolina used this date for their Memorial Day---not May 30th, which is the national holiday.

The ceremony was held on the Sunday closest to the tenth of May. All the boys and girls met at the Grammar School at the appointed hour, dressed in white, and carrying a bunch of flowers picked from their gardens. Some of the boys hated this, fearing that it was not masculine looking to carry flowers. They tried to get by with carrying only <u>one.</u> We marched, according to grades, down to Old Saint David's cemetery—with the surviving Civil War veterans leading the

3

parade. They solemnly carried the Confederate flags, which had been used in the various companies in which they had served. I remember the number gradually dwindled to three, then to one. The last veteran was Mr. Baker—the lone survivor to carry the banner.

A local minister opened the ceremony with a prayer. This was followed by a short address. Then---songs that the soldiers had sung around the campfire, sung by a heavenly quartet. It tore your heart just to listen to the words.

SCHOOL CHILDREN SCATTERING FLOWERS AROUND
THE MONUMENT PHOTO TAKEN IN 1950.

"Scatter Flowers" was the cue for the children to march around the monument, laying wreaths and flowers beneath it. At this time the older girls broke away and placed their flowers over the graves of unknown soldiers. Each year my sister Es and a few others were assigned a special veteran's grave to decorate. Her soldier's name was Mr. Brock. These rituals somehow personalized that War for all of us. After we had finished, the grown-ups repeated this laying of flowers at the monument.

The quartet was composed of Edwin McIver (*the same little boy who had sat on Sherman's lap and tried to feel the horns growing out of his forehead*), Mr. Willie Powell, John Evans and W. P. Pollock. Mr. Willie Powell sang the sweetest high tenor. I can see him now. As he approached the very highest notes, he would, ever so slowly, rise up on his toes.

The harmony of this quartet and the timbre of those voices melded together in perfection. And as Es said, "Their music was like a caress." You see, people were still grieving. Poignant stories had been handed down from one generation to the next. We all felt it. People were still in pain, weeping.

"After the peace, Confederate women were expected to retreat from the military stance of wartime duties and return to reappear in society as obedient and docile vessels. Many did, but this was a male sanctioned socio-political expectation, calculated to reclaiming masculine authority in the postwar era.

"The path Confederate women traveled to memorializing their military heroes culminated in the Lost Cause Movement."

Campbell ends her book with this tantalizing statement: "The cultural politics of war and memory reflected the interrelationship of race, sex, and the military. Together they linked Sherman and the white women of the South in an eternal war. This begs scholars to delve further into a fascinating unfolding historical saga: the truth about Confederate women and the roles they played during the Civil War."

A LITTLE BACKGROUND ON SHERMAN:

From *Sherman's March Through the Upper Pee Dee Region of South Carolina* by Larry E. Nelson

He was not anti-Southern. Not anti-slavery. He was pro-Union. He graduated from West Point, and had been posted at several places including Fort Moultrie in Charleston, a post in Louisiana and later in Tenn. and Mississippi. So he had friends in the South, and fond memories of the people there.

After marching through Georgia and burning Atlanta, Sherman led his army on the march to Savannah and then into the Carolinas. His objective during that campaign was to destroy the material capacity of the South by smashing as much confederate infrastructure as possible and to crush Southern morale by striking fear into Southern hearts. His troops systematically wrecked railroads, bridges, mills, gins, factories and public buildings. They consumed and destroyed immense quantities of foodstuffs and livestock. They visited the horrors of war upon civilians through plundering and pillaging farms, plantations, villages and towns. The devastation was catastrophic, and Southern morale plummeted.

The army reached Savannah shortly before Christmas of 1864—not destroying it. Sherman sent a message to Lincoln: "I beg to present to you as a Christmas gift the city of Savannah, with one hundred fifty heavy guns and plenty of ammunition, also about twenty five thousand bales of cotton."

Now, crossing the line into South Carolina was a different matter.

In spite of his long-ago fond memories there, Sherman now hated South Carolina because it was the first state that seceded from the Union. Remember, he was pro-Union. South Carolina was where the war began.

His soldiers were particularly eager to bring havoc on South Carolina Sherman remarked, "The truth is, the whole army is burning with an insatiable desire to wreck havoc on this state."

Everyone assumed he would head towards Charleston. Many people in Charleston and the Low country feared the worst, evacuated—and fled to Cheraw, only fifteen miles from the North Carolina border.

But just as he surprised everyone by not burning Savannah, he pulled off another surprise. Bypassing Charleston, his army marched to Columbia, the capital, leaving a trail of ruin. Within a matter of hours, much of the city was in flames. For the next two days, soldiers continued the work of destruction in and around Columbia, Orangeburg, Camden and Winnsboro. His orders were to move on to Fayetteville, North Carolina

From an article in *The State--Columbia Record*
(February 16-17, 1965).

Sherman's northward foray after leaving Columbia was yet another of a series of feints which enabled him to keep the Confederate defenders off balance. The direction of March indicated he might be moving towards the city of Charlotte, North Carolina. It was there that he hoped to obtain reinforcements and supplies and equipment for the men, who, by then would have marched four hundred twenty five miles from Savannah.

But he swung rather sharply to the east. Before him was the district of Chesterfield County and the town of Cheraw on the banks of the Great Pee Dee River. He wanted to get there before the Confederate army would burn that covered bridge so they could escape.

THE OLD COVERED BRIDGE – CHERAW, SOUTH CAROLINA
TAKEN AT THE TIME OF A FRESHET, SHOWING HOW HIGH THE RIVER
HAD RISEN. NOTICE THE SMALL TOLL HOUSE ON THE LEFT.

7

Terrible fighting happened there with the Confederate army. Thompson's Creek, Juniper Creek, Lynch's river etc.---(*all places I am familiar with and were swimming holes for my father's generation, before swimming pools came into vogue*). All were very close to Cheraw. Some of the more vicious atrocities of the whole Carolina march were reported at nearby Cash's Depot and Society Hill. (*As Mt. Pleasant is to Charleston, so is Society Hill and Cash's Depot to Cheraw.*)

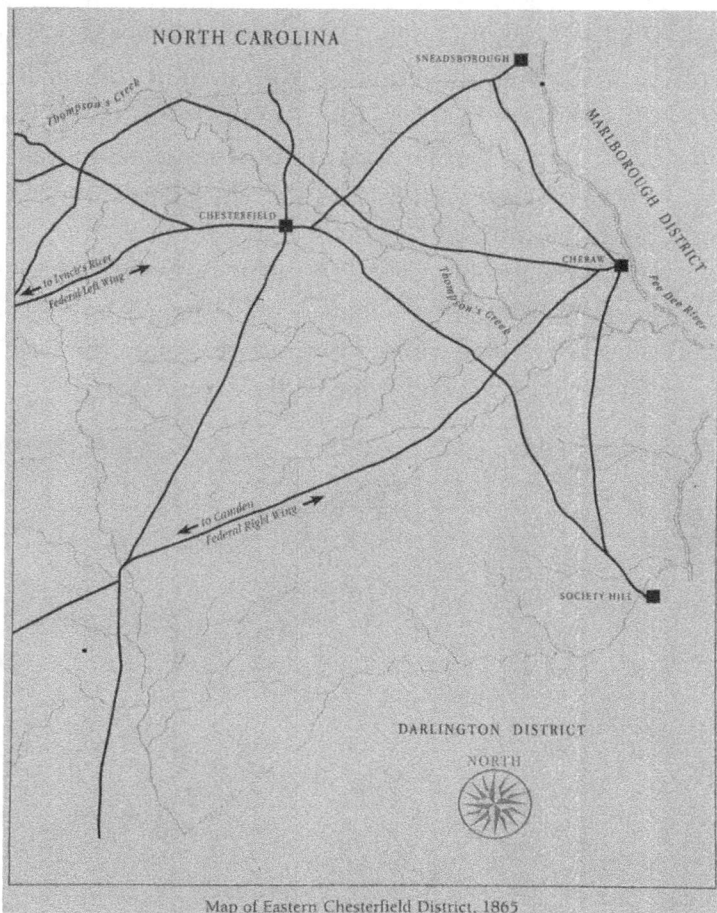

Map of Eastern Chesterfield District, 1865

CASH'S DEPOT WAS ABOUT 6 MILES SOUTH OF CHERAW AND ABOUT 4 MILES NORTH OF SOCIETY HILL

Taken from Jefferson Davis' book: *The Rise and Fall of the Confederate Government.*

Quotes from Rev. John Bachman's letter to Jefferson Davis:
(This is the Rev. John Bachman, Charleston's Lutheran minister, who was a close friend and collaborator with John James Audubon, famous ornithologist. Bachman's two daughters married Audubon's sons.)

"When Sherman's army came sweeping through Carolina, I happened to be at Cash's Depot, six miles from Cheraw. The owner of the Plantation there was a widow, Mrs. Ellerbe, 71 years of age. Her son, Col. Cash was absent. I witnessed the barbarities inflicted on the aged, the widow, and young and delicate females. Officers in high command were engaged in tearing from the ladies their watches, their earrings and wedding rings, the daguerreotypes of those they loved and cherished. They were compelled to strip before them to see if other valuables were concealed. A system of torture was practiced towards the weak, unarmed and defenseless. Before they arrived at a plantation, they inquired the names of the most faithful and trustworthy family servants. These were immediately seized, pistols pointed at their heads, and were threatened to be shot if they did not assist them in finding buried treasure.

"If they did not succeed, they were tied up and cruelly beaten. The last resort was that of hanging. Officers and men were engaged in erecting gallows and hanging up these faithful and devoted servants. They were strung up with the noose very tight and left there until life was nearly extinct, then let down, suffered to rest a while, then threatened and hung up again.

"I was the only male guardian of the refined and delicate females who had fled from the Lowcounty for shelter and protection. The first party that came was headed by officers. They were polite, saying that they were to secure our firearms, and that nothing in the house should be touched. Then they said they were authorized to press forage for their large army. I asked for a guard to protect the females. They said that there was no necessity for this, as the men dare not act contrary to orders.

"But the second and third parties followed immediately, demanding keys to bureau drawers, and gathered up jewelry, spoons, knives, forks, towels, tablecloths etc. Then they carted away elegant carriages and all vehicles on the premises. These were filled with bacon and plunder. The smokehouses were emptied and their contents carried off. Every head of poultry was seized and flung over their mules. Every article of harness which they did not want was cut in pieces.

"The fourth party came to burn and lay to ashes everything that was left. They swore they would make the damned rebel women pound their corn with rocks, and eat their raw meal without being able to cook it. I walked out at night, and the innumerable fires that were burning as far as the eye could reach illuminated the whole heavens, terrifying those that witnessed this destruction.

"My trials however were not yet over. I had already suffered much in a pecuniary point of view. I had been collecting a library on natural history during a long life. The most valuable of these books had been presented by various societies in England, France, Germany and Russia etc. who had honored me with membership. These works had never been for sale, and could not be purchased. They were detained in Columbia, and there the torch was applied and all were burned.

"I was now doomed to experience in person the effects of barbarous cruelty. The robbers had been informed in the neighborhood that the family which I was protecting had buried one hundred thousand dollars in gold and silver. They asked me where the money had been hid. I told them I knew nothing about it. They prepared to inflict torture on a defenseless gray-haired old man. They carried me behind a stable, and once again demanded where the money was buried. They cocked their pistols at my head. I told them to fire away. One of them kicked me in the stomach until I fell breathless and prostrate. As soon as I was able, I rose again. Once more he asked where the silver was. I answered as before. He kicked me on my back until I fell again. Thus I was either kicked or knocked down seven or eight times.

"Now", said he. "I'll try a new plan. How would you like to have both of your arms cut off?" With his heavy sheathed sword, struck me on my left arm, near the shoulder. I heard it crack. It hung powerless by my side and I supposed it was broken. He repeated the blow on the other arm. The pain was most excruciating.

"At that moment, the ladies, headed by my daughter, who had only then been made aware of the brutality practiced on me, rushed from the house, and came flying at my rescue. 'You dare not murder my father,' said my child. 'He has been a minister in the same church for fifty years, and God has always protected, and will protect him.' Miraculously they stopped, and walked away. The bravery of a young lady standing up to fierce army brutes, out of control, was astounding."

The following quotes from Lowcountry refugees in Society Hill are from the book *Sherman's March Through the Upper Pee Dee Region of South Carolina* by Larry E. Nelson.

More examples of women on the home front:

Anxiety was at a fever pitch. Most residents decided to remain in their homes to protect their houses and other real property. (If the soldiers came upon an unoccupied house it was burned immediately.)

Finding places of safekeeping for items that the foragers were likely to seize or destroy became a high priority. Concealing food, alcoholic beverages and valued personal belongings were primary concerns. One of the easiest ways to dispose of food was to eat it. Elizabeth Alston Pringle, who was nineteen and a refugee from a Lowcountry plantation (Chicora Wood outside of Georgetown) said, "We lived very high, and the things which we had preciously hoarded until the men of the family should come home were now eaten. Every day we had real Christmas dinner. All the turkeys and hams were used. We resorted to pouring the spirits and beverages into nearby streams."

To protect clothing and personal belongings, women sometimes wore two or three dresses and concealed valuables under their clothing. Again, Elizabeth Alston Pringle described such a procedure:

"We made long homespun bags, quite narrow, and with a strong waistband, and a strong button, to be worn under the skirts. And into these we put all our treasures. Our kind and generous neighbor, Mrs. Wm. Evans, was a very, very thin, tall woman. (*Her daughter married my great uncle Rob Godfrey.*) But when I ran over to see her she came out into the piazza to meet me, I could not believe my eyes. She seemed to be an enormously stout woman! I looked so startled that she said, 'My dear Bessie, they say these brutes take everything but what you have on and burn it before your eyes. So I have bags of supplies, rice and wheat flour and sugar and what little coffee we had, hung around my waist, and I have on all the clothes I can possibly stand.' We never got used to Mrs. Evans condition, but we each had treasures unknown to the others concealed about us."

In many instances, frightened occupants, usually women and children, shut themselves in a room while foragers ransacked the house, but some experienced quite a different response. Mrs. Evans of Society Hill reported: "I had feared before the Yankees came that I would have been intimidated, but strange to say, I met them without the slightest fear. A feeling of indignation and disgust overpowered all other emotions."

Elizabeth Pringle experienced a similar reaction when the Federals were in her family home. "It was odd how impossible it was not to follow them to see what they did. We were borne along to keep up with them and watch them. Whenever they asked me anything I answered with some quick, sharp speech which would intensely amuse anyone but the questioner, who generally relapsed into sulky silence."

Virginia Tarrh told of a friend "who sat knitting very complacently while the house was being searched, and had her watch concealed in the ball of knitting cotton. At the same time, she had a bag of flour slipped into each pillow case on the bed, and they escaped detection."

While whites typically resented the Union troops as invaders and oppressors, the response among blacks living in the area was more complex. Many blacks chose to help the Northerners and to break free from slavery. Slaves provided military information and revealed the hiding places of livestock and other valuable property. They seized the opportunity to escape from slavery by joining the train of refugees accompanying the Federal army. Some took with them as token compensation for unrequited toil personal valuables belonging to the former masters. But in other cases, the emotional ties of home transcended the cruel injustices of slavery, and some blacks decided to aid Southern whites. Slaves took horses and other livestock into the swamps and hid there until the troops had gone. Slaves warned the approach of foragers and otherwise assisted families with the trials of life under Federal occupation.

Quotes from *Sherman's March* by Burke Davis

Camden:

The heroine of Camden's town folk was Miss Sally Chestnut, a spinster who lived with her ninety three year old father in the stately plantation known as Mulberry. When a Federal officer entered and sat before the fire while the Chestnuts had breakfast, Sally said, "Rebels have no rights, but I suppose you have come to rob us. Please do so and go. Your presence agitates my blind old father." The enraged officer rose and shouted, "What do you take me for? A thief?" He stormed out empty handed.

To Mrs. Furman's consternation, one of Sherman's officers took a pretty mulatto girl of the neighborhood as his bride. One of the Yankee officers was married to her by a Roman Catholic priest and then demanded from Mrs. Yarborough her best bed to sleep on.

13

When the Federal horde had passed on, Mrs. Furman said, "There was a good deal of insubordination among the freed slaves who were left behind. Negroes took over several farms in the community from whites and divided the land among themselves in a bold step to taking possession of the property of their former masters."

Executions of foragers

The rape of another South Carolina white woman set off a savage exchange of executions and retaliations between Federals and Confederates. The rebel General James Chestnut who had stopped at a farmhouse for fodder for his horse, found that the owner had fled from home. The owner's wife found some fodder for him. Chestnut admired her daughter, a beautiful girl in her teens. "You should send her away," he told her. "You are in the track of the armies, and the stragglers will do anything."

The girl insisted on remaining with her mother. A squad of Wheeler's men brought news: The Confederates had reached that house in the afternoon to find the place in shambles. The girl was dead. Her mother was raving insanely—Federal soldiers had come, bound her hand and foot, and one after another, had raped her daughter.

Wheeler's troops took immediate and repulsive revenge. The rebel troops overtook the supposed raiders, killed them at once, cut their throats and left the twenty bodies at the roadside.

On February 22nd, eighteen of Kilpatrick's men were killed in this way, and on some of the bodies were crudely lettered messages: "Death to all Foragers."

In an effort to halt the murders, Sherman ordered his commanders to kill a Confederate soldier for each such Federal corpse they found. It became official army policy. Kilpatrick sent a message to Wheeler: "Unless some satisfactory explanation is made to me before sundown, February 23rd, I will cause eighteen of your men, now my prisoners, to be shot at that hour." And thus the retaliations began.

Back to our story of Sherman in Cheraw.

From *Sherman's March Through the Upper Pee Dee Region of South Carolina* by Larry E. Nelson.

Cheraw had commercial connections to the coast via the river and the railroad. Located in a cotton-growing district, Cheraw housed a considerable quantity of cotton that could not be shipped to world markets because of the naval blockade at the seacoast. It became a haven for refugees from the Lowcountry seeking safety from fighting along the seaboard.

The town was a depot for personal property because residents of the Lowcountry shipped into Cheraw for safekeeping everything from household furnishings to fine wines. The Confederate government also sent to the town a vast quantity of supplies, ranging from cannon to corn.

Sherman did not know the huge quantity of personal and public property in Cheraw. For him the chief attraction of the town was the covered bridge over the Pee Dee River.

Both wings of his army passed through the sleepy tree-lined village of Cheraw and found it an astonishing storehouse of treasure. Its warehouses, stables and sheds were bursting with valuables that had been shipped from Charleston for safety. The furniture, books, paintings and statuary accumulated by Charleston's wealthy families for generations was assembled here, and Sherman's "bummers," who were the first into the town, lost no time in falling upon the tempting loot.

Colonel Oscar Jackson, who had seen the army in its more lawless moods said, "Such stealing was astonishing even in the army. It beats Columbia in many respects."

Among the choice stores were cases of fine liquor, brandy and wine that had been shipped through the blockade. Jackson recorded their fate in his diary.

The best of the captured wine found its way to Sherman's head-quarters. His staff officers picked over the eight wagonloads of imported vintages. Sherman commented that the wine was the finest Madeira he had ever tasted.

The skirmishing was heavy as the Union troops entered the town with hopes of capturing the Pee Dee River Bridge before the Confederate army could burn it. The fighting was street-to-street and sometimes house-to-house. But the Confederate Army did manage to escape and burn the bridge, even as Yankee troops reached the entrance to the bridge. It was that close. Therefore Sherman's troops had to camp there on the Cheraw side of the river and build pontoon bridges to get them across. This explains the unexpected five day occupation of the town.

Cheraw ranked with Columbia and Fayetteville as the most important depots of Confederate supplies captured by Sherman during his march through Carolina.

The first day in Cheraw had been notable for its noise. Scores of Confederate cannon had been captured, including one bearing a brass plate: FIRST GUN FIRED ON FORT SUMTER—the cannon that had opened the Civil War! Sherman's gunners had fired twenty-three of the old guns in salute to President Lincoln, who was inaugurated for his second term in Washington during the day.

There were also a number of accidental explosions:

One veteran noted: "When we made a fire to cook our coffee there was a little flash of powder that ran along the ground and one yelled, 'Look out for the magazine!' We ran for cover. There was a tremendous explosion. Dirt and stones flew in every direction. Hundreds of soldiers were knocked to the earth, six soldiers and several civilians were killed and three houses were demolished as shot and shell rained over the city. A Confederate magazine had been destroyed.

General Sherman was thoroughly aroused, and was on the point of ordering the city reduced to ashes, and the Mayor and other city officials placed before a firing squad, before it was found that they weren't to blame.

Sherman's grim standing order that his officers take revenge for Confederate atrocities was carried out in a macabre scene in Cheraw, to the indignation of some of his troops. In camp near the town they found the body of one of its men, bearing the telltale rebel warning: DEATH TO FORAGERS. The victim was private Woodrough, a soldier who was not too popular with his mates.

Major William Rhodes, a regimental commander, at first refused to execute a Confederate prisoner in retaliation for the murder of Woodrough, and did not issue the order until Sherman threatened him with a court-martial.

A similar occasion happened at the junction of the Cheraw-Camden road and the Chesterfield-Society Hill road. A melancholy event occurred that troubled even battle hardened Northern soldiers. In accordance with standing instructions from Sherman, General Blair ordered his provost marshal to select a prisoner to be shot in retaliation for the murder of a Federal forager found beaten to death near Lynch's river. The prisoners cast lots and James M. Miller, who was forty-eight years old, drew the fatal lot. An infantryman from Wisconsin described the events that followed:

He was asked, "Do you have anything to say?" The old man's voice was flat and unhurried, "I was forced into the army. Never was in a battle. Never wished the Yankees any harm."

After a pause, he said, "I have nine children, all girls. I'm a Methodist preacher back home." Several of the Federal soldiers were blinking tears as the firing squad shuffled into place.

"The old man was blindfolded, placed with his back to a pine tree, and given a handkerchief to drop as a signal to the firing party. When all was ready, there were a few seconds of death—like stillness and suspense, every eye being riveted on the handkerchief in the old man's fingers; it fluttered to the ground—'Fire!' said the officer—and, as the smoke floated among the tall pines, our boys looked with sadness and sympathy upon the bleeding corpse of a brave old man who had met death unflinchingly and heroically for the crime of another man."

17

All of these rumors of executions reached Cheraw, building on the fright and anxiety as Sherman was bearing down on the last town in this hated state. Not only that, Cheraw was the largest town of the first county of the first state to secede from the Union. Everyone was terrified. The civilians in Cheraw and vicinity made preparations.

Now it would be up to the defenseless women to face this foe alone.

Frightened citizens stayed indoors, not knowing what to expect. To keep order, the provost patrolled the streets and sentries were posted at almost every home to protect the premises against unauthorized intrusion. Nonetheless, destruction and pillage were common.

Acting on orders, soldiers set fire to railroad facilities, public buildings and warehouses filled with corn. Other soldiers took it upon themselves to plunder and burn the business district. When the fires threatened to reach the Town Hall and other buildings serving as temporary hospitals, the Federal provost guard stopped the progress of the flames. The fires in Cheraw were visible as far away as Rockingham, North Carolina. In Chesterfield, Union troops burned the County Courthouse, destroying the building and all the records there.

A soldier's diary of impressions: (Dr. E. P. Burton)

"It was a very pretty town of some three or four thousand inhabitants. I stopped at the Baptist Church and played a tune on a melodeon. I went into the churchyard around the Episcopal Church—the church was an ancient building, said to have been used as a hospital by the British in the Revolutionary War."

Information Quoted from a Cheraw Brochure:

Old St. David's Church: Built in 1770. The last church built in South Carolina under the authority of King George III. In 1780 the church was used as headquarters for the 71st Highlanders, many of whom died here and were buried in a mass grave near the church doors.

In the cemetery around the church are buried soldiers from every war since the Revolution (although none of the stones date prior to 1820, the year steamboats began bringing gravestones up river from Charleston). The steeple and vestibule were added in 1826.

Confederate Monument: Cemetery, Old St. David's c. 1867. The first monument ever to be erected in memory of those who had fallen in the Confederate War. The inscription does not mention Confederate soldiers directly since Union forces still occupied the area.

A MODERN VIEW OF ST. DAVID'S CHURCH
DR. E.P. BURTON, THE FEDERAL SURGEON WHO VISITED ST. DAVID'S, CONSIDERED THE CHURCH "AN ANCIENT BUILDING" IN 1865.

From *All In One Southern Family, Volume II, Life in Cheraw*
edited by Adeline Godfrey Pringle Merrill:

THE CIVIL WAR IN CHERAW

It is a folk memory

The following stories and articles are a collection of experiences
of Cheraw citizens, and family members—all giving their
accounts of Sherman's Army in Cheraw.

It has been told that Mr. Conlaw P. Lynch, one of the few Catholics
in town, made an appointment to see General Sherman—himself a
Catholic. He took with him his little five year old daughter Marie,
and she is the one who begged the General to spare the town. *(Miss
Marie Lynch would become the aunt who raised her nephew, Lynch
Bellinger, the famous aviation pioneer hero.)*

Two men who played a role in this story of Sherman in Cheraw:

1. Judge Henry McIver. *(He married my grandmother's sister,
   Caroline Powe. Sherman took his meals at this house.)*

2. Chancellor John Inglis. He drafted the articles of Secession.

Two memoirs handed down to the Charles L. Prince family, courtesy of Laurence Lemprier Prince:

1. *Memoirs of Laura Prince Inglis* regarding her father's escape
   from Sherman. She was the daughter of Chancellor John
   Inglis.

2. *Memoirs of Charles L. Prince.* This is an account of his family's escape from Sherman's advance on Cheraw. He was a lad only eleven years old at the time. Charles Prince's father, General W.L.T. Prince, and his uncle, Chancellor J.S. Inglis played a major role in drawing up the Ordinance of Secession.

Quote from Laurence L. Prince, a classmate and friend of
Adeline Godfrey:

"A line in my grandfather's Memoirs indicated that it was through the aegis of the Godfreys that my people had a place to stay upon their return from the flight before Sherman's army. All their properties had been burned to the ground and they had nowhere to go."

TWO MEMOIRS

HANDED DOWN IN THE CHARLES L. PRINCE FAMILY

Courtesy of Laurence Lemprier Prince

PORTIONS OF THE MEMOIRS OF LAURA PRINCE INGLIS (UNMARRIED), DAUGHTER OF JOHN A. INGLIS AND LAURA PRINCE.

I first realized that the war had begun when I saw the troops in their gray uniforms, drilling in the streets of Cheraw. Col. E.B.C. Cash had raised the 8th regiment of South Carolina Volunteers. My eldest brother, Wm. C. Inglis, was Adjutant. I don't remember of how many companies the regiment was composed, but I think that most of the Cheraw men were in Company B. Dr. James Powe was the Captain.

After drilling for several months in the different towns, the State troops joined forces and all went into camp in Darlington County near Florence to learn the various military maneuvers, and the hardships of camp life. Their mothers, wives, sisters and daughters went down to Florence about twice a week laden with great baskets of tempting home food, and how gladly they welcomed us. About this time the Soldier's Aid Society was formed.

My mother was made President of the Society. They made uniforms, underwear, and flags, and knit hundreds of pairs of socks. I can never forget the day when almost the whole town went down to Florence to bid goodbye to our boys when the news came to us that all the State troops had been ordered to Virginia. It was tearing one's heart out, yet we had for their sakes to "put a cheerful courage on." A company of Infantry from just across the North Carolina line left for Virginia from our Cheraw depot, and most of the women in town went down to bid them goodbye. They called themselves the Yadkin Wild Cats. Among them was a young North Carolinian who had clerked for several years in one of our drug stores. I can't recall his name. He was a very small man, with a voice to match. Being the only man in the Company known to me, I said as I bid him goodbye, "Why Mr. ___ are you a Wild Cat?" "No'm. I'm a kitten" he replied in his meek little voice. It caused a laugh among all who heard him, which helped a lot.

Before hostilities had begun the Northern people were getting very nervous about the impending war. A noted public speaker addressing an immense audience in New York, in an effort to quiet their fears, said: "You needn't be at all alarmed, there will be no war, I assure you. Don't you know that those lazy, cowardly Southerners will run as soon as they see our brave New England soldiers." The first battle was the battle of Bull Run, and the Cheraw boys were in that battle. I've heard my brothers tell of it. It was funny to hear about it. After all their bragging, hats, coats, knapsacks, pistols, swords—in fact everything that impeded progress—was thrown away as they ran. There was little or no mention made in the Northern papers of this battle. The Confederate forces numbered 600,000 and for four years, they held at bay 2,778,333. Of this number, 494,000 were foreigners, and 186,017 were Negroes, and yet the Yankees brag about their great victory.

When the fighting had really begun, we, who were left at home, lived in a state of constant anxiety over so many dear to us. When our side won a battle, the conductor on the southbound train would have the whistle blown continuously from Thompson's Creek to Cheraw, and all the men left in town would be at the depot to meet it and hear the news. But the next morning was the trying time, when the newspapers came. Many of us dreaded to open them. When Yankee gunboats commenced to shell Charleston, the women and children were removed as promptly as possible, out of range, and the towns in the upper part of the state were crowded with refugees. My father sold our house to Mr. Joe Walker, of Charleston, the grandfather of Prentis Walker now living in Spartanburg. (*Walker, Evans & Cogswell Printing Co., corner of East Bay and Elliott St.*)

When Sherman's famous march to the sea was in progress and had reached the boundary line between Georgia and South Carolina, the late Chief Justice Henry McIver, then a Captain in Wade Hampton's brigade, sent a courier on horseback through the country, with a letter to my father urging him to get out of the line of Sherman's march at once, as he (Sherman) had offered a prize of $10,000 for his capture, and when captured he was to be hung, as an author of the Ordinance of Secession. It was only on my mother's earnest entreaty that he consented to act on Captain McIver's advice. When she reminded him of the rumors afloat as to the indignities offered young girls by Yankee soldiers, the question was settled. My mother ordered the carriage, packed a change of clothes for my father and myself, and we were off, taking my mother to town to stay with her mother until we returned. Then arrangements were made for Uncle Wm. Prince and my cousins Leslie and Annie Prince to accompany us. Willie and Charlie (*Laurence's grandfather*), both little boys, came along, each on horseback, thus saving two horses for Uncle William, and my father's two carriage horses were saved.

As this brings us up to when Charlie's reminiscences began, I will skip that part and instead will take this opportunity to explain ("for the benefit of my posterity") why neither Uncle William (*Laurence's great grandfather*) nor my father were in the military service of the Confederacy. Uncle William took the physical examination required, and was rejected as being unfit for military service on account of the feeble condition of his health. My father was a Judge in the Supreme Court of the State, and it was considered necessary that the work of the Courts should not be interrupted. They both did all they possibly could to forward the cause of the Confederacy.

The escape trip Charlie writes about lasted about a week. Then, we came home to find our home "the Woodlands" and Uncle William's

"Pine Grove" utterly destroyed, with all the contents. Nothing left but ashes and chimneys. My father's library of over four thousand volumes reduced to ashes. My five hundred dollar Steinway piano cut to pieces with axes, before starting the fire. The family portraits slit into ribbons with bayonets. Two of our Negroes followed the Yankees round from room to room and entreated them to spare our property, but their efforts were all in vain. They even took my clothes, laid them on the floor of the loom house, and ruined them by pouring white paint all over them. They stole all the horses and mules on the place and shot the cows, leaving their carcasses lying all about the yard. The Negroes were true to us and did all they could to help. During the week of our absence, the atrocities and outrages committed by Sherman's army were past belief. During the second year of the war, the pews in the Presbyterian Church had been removed and the building used as a hospital for any sick or wounded who were able to get back. The first Sunday of Sherman's occupation of the town they had a ball that night in the church, the fiddlers etc. were in the pulpit, and the floor filled with Yankee soldiers dancing with Negro women. The town was overrun with the pests, forcing their way into every house, breaking open trunks and bureau drawers and stealing all the valuables that they wanted.

When they came to Grandma's (*Charlotte Prince—Laurence's great grandmother*) they walked all through the house, into private rooms occupied by members of the family, in no instance asking permission. After they had pillaged every upstairs room and reached the one in which the trunks of different members of the family were stored, the officer in charge of the "gang" sent for "the lady of the house to come to them." My mother, to spare her mother, went up and found the trunk room a scene of utter confusion—every trunk broken open and the contents scattered all over the floor.

Among the trunks was a large wooden box, about the size of the wardrobe trunk of today. It had iron bands over the top, like the usual leather straps to trunks, iron handles at each end, and fastened with an iron padlock. It was so heavy it required four men to lift it. This box and seven trunks belonged to my father's aunt, an unmarried woman of over eighty years of age, who had supported herself for several years as principal of a girl's college at Hagerstown, Md. My father, considering her too old to look out for herself went to Md. and brought her down to take care of her in our home. With her she brought nine trunks, including the box. When war seemed inevitable she insisted on returning to Md. Being a rigid Episcopalian, my father took her to the Episcopal Home for the aged. She took only one of her trunks.

To go back to the box, when my mother entered the room, the officer in charge asked her what was in that box. She replied, "I have no idea. It belongs to an old lady, my husband's aunt." His reply to that was "That's a lie, you do know." My mother's answer to that was, "Well, I am an unprotected woman, with no man present to resent that insult, but you took the liberty to open all the others, why not this?" The reply was that they had tried and couldn't open it. Said it was so heavy that he was sure it was filled with arms and ammunition. So they went to work to try again to open it, cursing and swearing and sweating until at last one of the men suggested, "Why not split it open with an axe?" This suggestion was eagerly acted upon. One of the men went down to the yard, found an axe and split the box in half, only to find it filled to the top with Episcopal Churchman Hymnals! My mother said she felt amply repaid for the insult offered her, when she saw the chagrin and disgust on the faces of the men who had spent their strength for naught, and their labor for that which profited not. She had to go into the next room to laugh. And enjoyed it.

Some of the atrocities committed by so called men against helpless women and young girls are past belief and not fit to be written. But some of the incidents, though, were rather funny. For instance, Rev. Dr. Taylor, the Methodist minister, kind and helpful and beloved by the whole town, made it his business to go, from day to day, to the homes in town left unprotected, to inquire if there was anything he could do to help them. One day he went to Col. MacFarland's (*Alex*

Quattlebaum's ancestor), the rich man of the town, a very kind and generous one too. When he rang the bell Mrs. MacFarland herself came to the door. When Dr. Taylor asked if there was any help he could render her, she whispered, "Yes" and drew him inside the door very quietly, and told him there was a Yankee upstairs rifling her bureau drawers of all jewelry and other valuables, and she wanted the doctor to walk up very quietly behind him, seize his hands, draw his arms behind him and hold him tight, and she would do the rest. Both of them were sturdy, well-built people. So the doctor grasped the thief's elbows, drew them behind him and held them as in a vice. Then Mrs. MacFarland went in front of him and slapped his jaws with all her might until she was so tired she had to stop. Dr. Taylor put the man out of the house and he and she had a good laugh over their performance.

THE JOHN INGLIS HOUSE WHERE THE TRUNKS WERE
PHOTO FROM LARRY NELSON'S BOOK: *SHERMAN'S MARCH THROUGH THE UPPER PEE DEE REGION OF SOUTH CAROLINA*

One of the saddest things I can recall in connection with those trying times was seeing our boys coming home after the surrender. They had gone out buoyant and full of hope, with never a thought of the possibility of defeat. I think most of the infantry came home on the train. Those that rung our hearts were Artillery and Calvary, who entered the town by way of Kershaw Street. They came at intervals in groups of from five to twenty-five, riding very slowly. Even the horses looked discouraged. We, having no other place of refuge, were still living at Grandma's, and we younger ones spent most of our time on the back piazza watching for any boys we might know. At last one stopped and brought a note from Charley Inglis, my brother, telling us to expect him about dusk. So I kept watch, and after what seemed to me quite an hour, another batch of ten or fifteen rode, and stopped at the back gate. One unlatched the gate, waving goodbye to the others who rode on, came in, carefully catching the gate again, rode up to the steps, dismounted and came up the steps. I had not seen my brother for more than a year and the dusk was upon us. So, nothing doubting, I fairly flew to meet him, squeezed him round the neck just as tight as I could, saying "Oh, Charley, I'm so thankful to have you safe at home once more." He gave me a nice, gentle little hug, patted my shoulder, and with a quiet laugh said, "I'm sorry but it isn't Charley." As he loosened his hold on me I stepped back and looking up in his face, saw I had been embracing a man whom I never saw before, nor have I ever seen him since. I was only sixteen then and seeing my embarrassment he was very kind in trying to put me at ease again. He said he and Charley were in the same company and were great friends, that Charley had invited him to stay with us that night and have breakfast before he rode to his home in Darlington. Uncle Wm. came out on the piazza about that time and took charge of him while I still waited for my brother, and when at last he did come and clasped me in his arms and kissed me over and over, I tell you, I felt the difference.

Reminiscences or Remnants of Recollection

Written by Charles L. Prince,
Son of William L.T. and Mary P. Prince
Cheraw, South Carolina
Baltimore Md., September 26th, 1931

In 1865 I was eleven years old, and was the youngest one of a party of eight (counting Robert, the Negro driver) who left Cheraw just before Sherman, with his eighty thousand Huns, entered it. Of this party there are only two of us left, Cousin Laura Inglis and myself.

My father was a member of the legislature in 1860. It was in session when Lincoln was elected President. The convention was called that took the State out of the Union. My uncle, Chancellor J.A. Inglis, was made Chairman of the committee to draw up the Ordinance of Secession, but when they were retiring for that purpose, Judge Wardlaw handed a paper to Judge Inglis with the remark, "See how that will do." The Committee read it over, and adopted it without a change. Judge Inglis, as chairman, offered it and it was carried without a single dissenting voice. So, South Carolina had exercised her constitutional right to secede from the Union. In December 1860 President Buchanan stated to Congress, "that no part of the Federal Government had the power to make war upon a state." In a history of North Carolina by that grand old Confederate, Captain S.A. Ashe, we find that the decision of the United States Supreme Court in December, 1862 was that, "By the Constitution, Congress, alone, has the power to declare a national or foreign war; the President has no power to institute or declare war against either a foreign nation or a domestic State." We have seen that Abe Lincoln committed this very act, when he issued his War Proclamation against the seceding states, without the consent of Congress or his Cabinet.

I knew nothing of this plan for going away, and had driven a one-horse wagon out home to bring in a load of light furniture.

When I started to town I could hear Sherman's musketry in the distance. There was great excitement on the road, and couriers on horseback were shouting, "Sherman is coming!" When I drove in the back gate, my mother was on the steps. She told me that Pa and the girls (Sister Annie, Cousin Leslie Prince and Cousin Laura Inglis) had gone. Father had left word for me to take the horse out of the wagon, saddle him, and follow them across the river—taking the road to Rockingham, North Carolina Brother Willie had gone with them on horseback. My mother took me in her arms, and bade me "goodbye" with tears streaming down her cheeks. When I rode down the street, the road was crowded with soldiers and cannon. Hardee's army was retreating before Sherman. When I reached the river bridge it was so crowded that I had to put my feet up on my horse's neck to keep from being rubbed. About a mile on the other side I met Brother Laurence, with his gray uniform trimmed with red. He said he was going home for an extra pair of trousers. I told him I didn't think he could get over, for they were preparing to burn the bridge when I crossed. He said he would try it, but the bridge was burning when he got there. Four or five miles further on I overtook my party. Robert, the Negro, was driver of the two-horse carriage with the three girls in it. The rockaway was driven by Pa. Uncle John Inglis was with him. Brother Willie and I brought up the rear on horseback.

We spent the night in Rockingham with Mrs. Covington—she insisting that we stay there and not go to the hotel. That night we could see the reflection of Cheraw burning. We didn't know but that the whole town was burning, and, of course, were very much worried about the dear ones left behind. But we learned afterwards that it was a few stores on Front Street, and they set fire to the magazine. The explosion shattered the windows of many houses and killed several Yankees. This magazine was an old brick house, situated in the ravine just off Front Street, about halfway between Market and Church Streets.

A Week Later:

Leaving Concord we were now heading for home. I haven't the slightest recollection of anything until we reached Cheraw. Owing to the terrible condition of the roads, and the tired horses, it must have taken us two or three days, but I don't remember what towns we passed through or anything about the trip. I do remember that as we neared Cheraw the roads were almost impassable. There were a great number of dead horses and mules, some of which had to be dragged out of the road.

We found our house nothing but a pile of ashes, and the Negroes camping on the roadside. We found our people all safe, and were delighted to be with them again. We were told that the Yankees, at first, intended to blow up Grandma's house and placed a keg of powder in the cellar. So they moved her (*Laurence's great, great grandmother, then eighty two years old*) some distance up the street---'twas said, in a wheelbarrow. She was two and one half square blocks from her house, and had not been out of the house for several years.

A Col. Russell decided to take the house for his headquarters. He put all the family in one room and took possession of all the rest of the house. Fortunately the family had a ham baked, and a lot of biscuits. They lived on this the five days the Yankees were in town. They had no place to cook, nothing to cook, because the Yankees had robbed them of everything. Ma said that none of the private soldiers that she saw around the place could speak English. They were Germans.

The town and the country for miles around were devastated, the conditions indescribable. I am not going to attempt to tell how we suffered for food. After Sherman left, for some time we lived on parched corn. I remember the first piece of bacon we got. We were living at that time out at the Godfrey summerhouse. Brother Willie had ridden into town and Pa had gotten a shoulder of bacon from a North Carolina wagon and had sent it home by him. I can see him now with his horse in a full run, waving the meat over his head. There was great excitement in that house. We were almost crazy. Occasionally we would kill a rabbit or squirrel, but ammunition was scarce. Many a shell I opened at risk of my life, to get the powder out of it. We would find lots of minnie balls which we could melt into strips and cut in pieces, for shot.

We lived in a number of houses—good people taking us in, for we had nothing. Everything was destroyed. After Grandma died we settled down in the old home in town. (*Now known as the Prince-Stevenson house.*)

MEMORIES OF MISS LAURA INGLIS

By Thomasine McCown Haynes

I was especially blessed to have had Miss Laura Inglis spend her last eight years as a member of our family because she told me so much about life in Cheraw before, during and after The War Between the States. She made me call it that for she said, "It was the most Un-Civil War ever fought." Some have referred to it as "the late unpleasantness," but from what Miss Laura reported, unpleasantness is the understatement of the century.

She told me how Southern Ladies would either have a servant do this, or they would—gather the uneaten corn dropped from the mouths of Yankee horses, wash and boil it, for food. The Yankees had either stolen or destroyed everything that was edible.

She did not have a teacher but received her education from her father in his law office in his home. She said he had the most extensive library in South Carolina. This was the office Sherman destroyed. Her father also shared an office with Judge McIver. Did I tell you about a trial, reported in an old history book of Marboro County, when the owner of a large plantation was hanged in Bennettsville for murdering his slave? The two lawyers were law partners, McIver and

Inglis, of Cheraw. Inglis represented the defendant and said when he heard the evidence presented by an impassioned McIver, he "trembled for his client." I have a photo copy of that account. Bobby Hanna told me that his father had some of Judge Inglis's law books and that he donated them to the University of South Carolina. So these law books evidently escaped Sherman's torch by being housed in the little law office downtown.

Some of her stories about Sherman's occupation of Cheraw were quite lurid. She told of two young ladies being forced to disrobe and play the piano for Yankee soldiers. "You'll never hear about that because Southern ladies would never disclose such public humiliation." Then she would fume, "I'm afraid I'm going to Hell. The Bible says you must love your enemies but I hate Sherman."

The Yankees burned their plantation home on the old Camden road, where her father had the largest collection of books in South Carolina. They slashed family portraits, slashed open the bedding and poured molasses into the beds, shot and killed all livestock before burning the house, barn and all buildings on the place.

Her father had a price on his head of ten thousand dollars (dead or alive) because he drew up the first rough draft of the Articles of Secession. Someone in Wade Hampton's Company rode on horseback to bring him the message that he must get out of town—that Sherman was heading towards Cheraw. His wife also insisted that he flee. When he left, he took little Laura with him. His wife remained behind, in their town house (*where Harriet Watts Stewart lived on Third Street*).

That home was searched and that is where more bedding was slashed open, molasses poured into the mattresses. Also, this is where that old trunk was found—so heavy that the Yankees could not lift it or open it. They suspected guns and ammunition were inside. Finding no key, an axe was brought and the trunk chopped open. It was filled with old Episcopal Hymnals!

Copied from an article in *The State* titled "Our Women in the War"

Sherman's Raiders in Cheraw

By Mrs. H. E. Godfrey (*Ad's grandmother*)

As I look back on the terrible years of our war, so many events crowd on my memory that it is difficult to separate...

But to give our younger friends some idea of the privations and suffering of that time I will speak of the (?) that Sherman and his eighty thousand men were here for five days and on the condition in which he left us.

When our Confederate army was here, General Stewart Elliott, of Fort Sumter fame, and his staff were guests of my father (Thomas Ellerbe Powe). As the scouts reported that Sherman would be here on Friday, on the night of the second of March, 1865, he advised my father to send me into town, that being Cheraw, as at that time we were living about a mile and a half from Cheraw on the Plantation. He advised this, as the Federal army pretended to have guards in town, while in the country there was not even the pretense. (My husband was a prisoner at Johnson's Island, so I was staying with my father.) At 12:00 o'clock my dear old father kissed me and my baby good-bye, both of us wondering under what conditions we would meet again. On my way to town, before we had left our own premises, we were halted. This seemed rather strange to me. But thankfully, the permit the General had given me carried me safely by our sentinels.

The next day, my sister-in-law, Claudia Godfrey, and I were out in the yard when there was such a patter on the leaves. We wondered whence the rain came, as the sky was cloudless, when we realized it was a shower of minnie balls, and immediately the streets were filled with bluecoats. They seemed to have sprung from the ground.

The bluecoats rushed into houses demanding keys, and when they were not forthcoming, broke open doors with their gunstocks.

They chased and beheaded every fowl in the yards, and pantries and cupboards were emptied. In the country, where they did not co-operate, they destroyed everything. Four times my father's house was set on fire, which faithful Negroes extinguished. General Conkling had his headquarters at my father's house, and gave a ball there the Saturday night he occupied the house.

It was soon discovered who the confidential servants were, and they were forced at the point of bayonet and rope's end, to tell where the valuables were hidden.

Those five days were my idea of hell. We were helpless and in the power of an immense body of soldiers.

During their stay two of the eight officers in the house asked me to play the piano and sing for them, and they selected all the songs. I did not play those. Instead, I played "Bonnie Blue Flag" and "My Maryland" etc. and I was expecting a bullet to be put through my head at any minute.

The following Thursday I went home to my father's plantation, "The Homestead," and I could then account for the heavy smoke we had seen in this direction. Gin house, stables, mill and hundreds of bales of cotton had all disappeared.

My dear old father met me without a coat on. They had taken it from him. In our house there was not a cup, plate, knife, fork, bed nor pillow could be found. Not a garment or mirror. The very books were destroyed.

My young readers will be interested to know I wore a wedding ring but eighteen months, for they took it. And not a piece of jewelry did I save. And they put my bridal veil on a mule's head and rode off with it.

For days we lived on the corn picked up in the deserted camp. This we boiled in ashes and seasoned with salt which was procured by digging up the dirt in the smoke houses, pouring water on it and letting the dirt settle. General Sherman had his headquarters in the yard of Mr. J.F. Matheson. (Tents were pitched over a great expanse of land there.) But he took his meals in my sister's house (Caroline and Chief Justice Henry McIver). He called the younger children at every meal to eat with him, which was a great relief to my poor sister, who had nothing for them.

SHERMAN'S HEADQUARTERS

J.F. MATHESON HOUSE
SHERMAN'S TROOPS PITCHED TENTS OVER A LARGE EXPANSE OF LAND HERE. BUT SHERMAN TOOK HIS MEALS IN THE POWE-MCIVER HOUSE SHOWN IN THE ABOVE PHOTOGRAPH.

Comments from Ad:

The story goes that Sherman was crazy about little Eddie McIver. He would sit Eddie on his lap. The little boy would reach up and feel and rub the General's forehead. Sherman asked him what he was doing. "I'm feeling for your horns."

The image of Sherman holding Eddie on his lap makes me think of yet another instance like that. When Sherman first arrived in Cheraw, Mr. Conlaw Lynch, one of the few Catholics in town, made an appointment to see Sherman—himself a Catholic. He took with him his little five year old daughter, Marie, and she sat on his lap and is the one who begged Sherman to spare the town.

This shows the ambivalence of Sherman—the gentle Sherman versus the cruel one. In this study I have been struck with Sherman's ambivalence: His cruelty, the way he mercilessly inflicted punishment on civilians, and yet at times he seemed thoughtful, kind and gentle.

Burke Davis wrote that his ambivalence in the matter of troop discipline stemmed from his conflicting beliefs that war must be made so terrible as to demoralize the enemy—but that troops should never be permitted to victimize the innocent and helpless. These problems would haunt him until the war's end.

Yet he had serious disciplinary problems, for he found it impossible to halt the pillaging of his troops. He vacillated back and forth.

From *Memoirs of Wm. T. Sherman*:
(Found in Ada Evans Stevenson's papers.)

"On the second of March we entered the Village of Chesterfield, skirmishing with Batters Cavalry, which gave ground rapidly. There I received a message from General Howard that he was already in Cheraw with the 17th Corps, and that the 15th was near at hand.

General Hardee has retreated east ward across the Pee Dee burning the bridge. Early in the morning of the 3rd of March I rode out of Chesterfield along with the 20th Corps, which filled the roads, forded Thompson's Creek, and at the top of the hill beyond, found a road branching off to the right which corresponded with the one on my map leading to Cheraw.

We reached Cheraw in a couple of hours in a drizzling rain, and while waiting for our wagons to come up, I stayed with General Blair in a large house, the property of a blockade-runner, whose family remained. General Howard occupied another house farther down the road (*the Nock house*). He had already ordered his pontoon bridge to be laid across the Pee Dee, there a large, deep, navigable stream, and Mowers division was already across, skirmishing with the enemy about two miles out. Cheraw was found to be full of stores which had been sent up from Charleston prior to its evacuation, and which could not be removed. The day was so wet that we all kept indoors; and about noon General Blair invited us to take lunch with him. We passed down into the basement dining room, where the regular family table was spread with an excellent meal; and during the progress I was asked to take some wine which stood upon the table in venerable bottles. It was very good and I inquired where it came from. General Blair simply asked, "Do you like it?" But I insisted on knowing where he had gotten it; he only replied by asking if I liked it and wanted some. He afterwards sent to my Bivouac a case containing a dozen bottles of the finest Maderia I ever tasted; and I learned that he had captured in Cheraw, the wine of some of the old aristocratic families of Charleston, who had sent it up to Cheraw for safety, and heard afterwards that Blair had found eight wagon loads of this wine, which he distributed to the army generally, in very fair proportions.

After finishing our lunch, as we passed out of the dining room Gen. Blair asked me if I did not want some saddle blankets, or a rug for my tent and leading me into the hall to a space under the stairway, he pointed out a pile of carpets which had also been sent up from Charleston for safety. After our headquarters wagon got up, and staggering under a load of Carpets, out of which the officer and escort made excellent tent rugs, saddle cloths, and blankets. There was an immense amount of stores in Cheraw, which were used or destroyed. Among them 24 guns, 2000 muskets, and 3500 barrels of gun powder. By the carelessness of a soldier, an immense pile of their powder was exploded, which shook the town badly, and killed and maimed several of our men.

We remained in or near Cheraw till the 6th of March, by which time the army was mostly across the Pee Dee River, and was prepared to resume the March on Fayettsville."

William T. Sherman

THE TENTH OF MAY

THE QUARTET – TAKEN AROUND 1900 – LEFT TO RIGHT:
MR. WILLIE POWELL, TENOR; EDWARD MCIVER "EDDIE";
W.P. POLLOCK "WILL"; JOHN EVANS, BASS (ADA'S FATHER)
PHOTO COURTESY OF ADA EVANS STEVENSON

Songs sung by the quartet at the tenth of May ceremonies, CHERAW

Tenting Tonight

We're tenting tonight on the old Camp
ground. Give us a song to cheer
Our weary hearts, a song of home,
And friends we love so dear.

Many are the hearts that are weary tonight,
Waiting for the war to cease;
Many are the hearts, looking for the right
To see the dawn of peace.
Chorus:
Tenting tonight, tenting tonight
Tenting on the old Camp Ground.
Last Chorus: Dying tonight, dying tonight,
Dying on the old Camp Ground.

Just Before the Battle, Mother

Just before the battle, Mother
I am thinking most of you,
While upon the field we're watching
With the enemy in view.

Comrades brave are round me lying;
Fill'd with tho'ts of home and God;
For well they know, that on the morrow,
Some will sleep beneath the sod.
Chorus:
Fare-well Mother, you may never
(a marvelous bass part)—You may never, you may nev-
er, Mother
Press me to your heart again;
But O, you'll not forget me, Mother
(again, that bass part)—you'll not forget me, Mother
If I'm number'd with the slain.

Let Us Pass Over the River
(Stonewall Jackson's last words.)

(There is a first part. I can hum it, but cannot think of the words.)
hough the dark waves roll high
We shall be undismayed
Let us pass over the river and rest under the shade
Rest under the shade
Rest under the shade of the tree.

CEREMONY ON THE 10TH OF MAY c. 1900.
WRITTEN ON THE BACK OF THIS PHOTO: "SAL – WHO IS
THE OLD BASTARD WHO DIDN'T TAKE OFF HIS HAT?"
SIGNED – McIVER EVANS
PHOTO COURTESY OF ADA EVANS STEVENSON

In more recent years the veterans have been joined by veterans of World War I and II, and the State Home Guard. In the shade of the monument are buried veterans from every war from the Revolutionary War through World War II.

It was a pretty sight to see the whole town walking past the town green and down the shady streets to the old church where all their dead lay under the great elms and oaks. It gave one a reverential feeling. Time, and the benign faith and love of those buried there, and of those who had buried them, transformed the place and hallowed it. People lowered their voices when they came inside the iron fence, and ceased talking altogether by the time they reached the church and the monument.

The Confederate Monument Cheraw, South Carolina

From United Daughters of the Confederacy (U.D.C.) papers loaned to me by "Sis" Huntley Hoover.

Confederate Monument, erected in 1867. Standing in the southeast corner of St. David's cemetery is the first Confederate monument ever erected.

The Confederate Veteran, a magazine published in Nashville, Tenn., made a canvas of the South in 1890 to determine which was the first monument; and after a year's search, they designated the Cheraw monument as the first one.

It has been said that it seemed especially fitting that the State of South Carolina and the town of Cheraw should have the honor to erect the first Confederate monument, since history shows the prominent place that our state had in the Confederacy. Cheraw, more than any other southern community, with the exception of New Orleans, Atlanta and Columbia suffered from the direct ravages of the war. It was here that all of Sherman's army congregated for five interminable days of horror and devastation.

In March of 1866, while Cheraw was at its lowest ebb financially but on the crest of the waves of patriotism and spirituality, a letter was received from Mrs. C.J. Williams of Atlanta, Ga. Mrs. Williams wrote this letter to various Soldier's Aid Societies saying: "We cannot

43

erect monumental shafts to the memory of our dead, but we can set aside one day in the year to cover their graves with flowers in token of our gratitude for their sacrifice." The head of the Soldiers Aid Society of Cheraw was Mrs. George Hearsey. In reading Mrs. Williams' letter to the meeting of their society, she said, "We not only can, but will erect a monument." Immediately the Ladies Memorial Association was organized. By the most unbelievable sacrifices, hard work and ingenuity, in June of 1867 a monument was unveiled in Cheraw to the memory of the Soldiers of the Confederacy. Judge Hudson of Bennettsville made the address to a large concourse of patriots---crippled, broken men and noble war-worn women.

Although the monument was erected "to the memory of the Soldiers of the Confederacy," these words could not be put on the monument. At the time the monument was erected, a Yankee garrison was still in Cheraw. The Yankees objected to any wording which would glorify the Confederate soldiers, but finally approved of the association's using the following words: "To the heroic dead who died at Cheraw."

They bought the monument from Mr. J.H. Villenauve, the marble cutter of Cheraw, who gave as his contribution the carving of the monument.

Mrs. Lillian Huntley's Notes – U.D.C. Chapter, Cheraw

On September 1, 1896 the Cheraw Chapter UDC held its first meeting at the home of Mrs. J.C. Coit. A band of nineteen loyal women applied for a chapter.

The fires of war were still burning in the hearts of these women, and their organization was to preserve for future generations the honor and bravery of these men who fought and died for a cause defeated but not conquered.

(The children who were taught by Miss Mattie Duvall, Mrs. Hartzell and Mrs. Margaret Godfrey Thrower were told so much of Confederate history that it must linger ever in their minds.)

Quote from a letter from Uncle Willie Godfrey:

"I never will get over the fact that Ma would not let me go fishing on the Tenth of May. 'Think of the poor soldiers,' she said, and made me feel like a culprit, to want to fish on Memorial Day."

Quote from a letter from Sarah Spruill, Cheraw—
October 2, 1990:

"Dear Ad,

We have enjoyed watching Ken Burn's Civil War series on TV—though I wish they had touched on some other things, and not emphasized some as much as they did. I am the last generation that will remember marching to the Confederate Monument. The practice was discontinued while I was in Grammar School in Darlington. In a way, I'm glad, because it symbolizes that the War, after a mere one hundred years or so is over."

(The Civil Rights movement of the 1960s certainly played a role, but the banning of this ceremony was long overdue.)

AFTERMATH

Told in Family Letters

FAMILY LETTERS WRITTEN DURING AND
AFTER THE WAR

Quotes from *Sherman's March Through the Upper Pee Dee
Region of SC*
By Larry Nelson

Because Sherman's troops had totally disrupted the means of trans-
portation and communication, civilians in the wake of the army were
isolated from the outside world. The isolation served to intensify
anxieties as people wondered about the fate of loved ones elsewhere
in the Confederacy. Emma Pringle in Society Hill penned a note on
March 30, 1865, to her sister in Augusta, Ga. "My dear Eliza. . .We
have no mails, now, either to, or from this remote corner. I write this
with the hope that it may reach you. .And I hope you may be able to
find some way of sending me news of you all, for I am very anxious to
know something of those I love so dearly."

By the same token, people in other places worried about friends
and family in the region ravaged by the advancing Federals. John
Evans had not received his wife Annie's letter of Feb. 22 when he
wrote to her on March 5th from Petersburg, Va.

"You can't imagine my anxiety about you at this time. We hear
rumors of the occupations of Cheraw by the enemy, and if so there is
no telling how many privations you are enduring."

From Entrenchments—Petersburg, or rather Picket line March 7th, 1865:

John Evans wrote: "My anxiety on your account is very great as we hear that our army is at Cheraw and that there has been a battle fought near you."

And yet again on March 16th, 1865:

"I hear that Cheraw has been entirely destroyed. If I could only know that you are all alive and suffered no bodily harm, I would be so glad, but here I am without one word from you since 24th Feb."

Letter from Ad's great-aunt Josephine Pritchard to a friend:
"Cheraw, SC May, 1868

I have a little school which I teach in a little house in the yard. Have ten scholars and would like to have many more, but since the war, so many female teachers have sprung up that there are almost as many teachers as there are students.

I lost everything with the Cause. I had about 5,000 dollars in Planters' Notes and Confederate Bonds, and not one dollar of which is good. So have nothing but what I make. But am thankful that I have health and strength. The rest of the family are very much reduced. Indeed, everyone is. The Robbins family has nothing.

Claudius Pritchard, my brother, is living in Camden. Like me he lost everything: the savings of 20 years, which had been laid aside to educate his children, and now that they are just at the age to need it, it is gone.

It would grieve you to see how our rich planters are reduced. The family of Gen. Gillespie, for instance. His nice house was burned by Sherman. (They lived in the country. Therefore his house was not protected or guarded.) He lives in a small summer house. His wife Mary does the cooking and sewing. Oliver milks the cows and Sam gets and cuts the wood. They have no servant at all.

I must not forget to tell you about Sherman's visit. We had the horrid creatures for five days, burning and plundering all the time. The whole of Front Street was burnt except Mr. Turner's store. It was occupied by a family of refugees. (All occupied houses were spared.)

Our very old church was very much injured by an explosion of gun powder. Before retreating, our army threw our gun powder (which was stored in the brick store) in the ravine back of the store. The church, being so near, was very much injured by this explosion. The walls are forced out several inches. The Yankees stole the heaviest pieces of our Communion set---the paten and tankard.

(Incidentally, we have a very promising young minister now. Rev. Mr. Motte—a lineal descendant of Rebecca Motte of Revolutionary memory---who gave the arrows to set fire to her house in which the British were quartered.)"

THE WILLIAM GODFREY HOUSE ON CHURCH ST.

FAMILY SIDEBOARD WHERE THE CHURCH SILVER
WAS PLACED. NOW IN THE DARGAN FAMILY.

Quoted from letter from Cora Page Godfrey to Adeline
Godfrey Merrill:

William Godfrey (*our great-grandfather*) was cashier of the old
Merchant Bank. He worked his way up to become President of that
bank, which eventually became known as the last Bank in the State
that honored Confederate money. After he became President he
then built his home on Church Street in the 1850's. It was at that
house that part of the St. David's communion silver was kept during
Sherman's occupation of Cheraw. This silver was divided between the
two Wardens of the church. William Godfrey placed his portion in a
sideboard in the dining room and it was not disturbed. Of course,
that house was protected by guards at the order of the Union Officer
who had been at West Point with Uncle Jimmy (*Grandma's brother*).

The other church warden, <u>Thomas Ellerbe Powe,</u> took his portion of the silver to his Plantation, The Homestead, which was just across Hucklebury Creek. It was buried near a spring. It was stolen and that farm was pretty well desolate. Grandma (*Harriet Powe Godfrey)* was staying there with her father while her husband, S.G. Godfrey, was imprisoned at Johnson Island—Sanducky, Ohio. Her father had anticipated trouble with the Federal troops and that is why he sent Grandma and her little daughter Margaret to town for protection at her father-in-law, William Godfrey's home on Church Street.

"The Homestead"---the second house built at Orange Hill—was built by Erasmus Powe. When Erasmus' widow, Esther Ellerbe Powe died, this house went to their son, Dr. Thomas Ellerbe Powe. This is where he was raised. It was at this plantation that he took his portion of the church silver to hide. He buried it near a stream. The Yankees found it and it was stolen. Dr. Powe was the father of Harriet. As a young girl she enjoyed horseback riding and jumping the fences with the horses out at this plantation.

Sherman's men did great damage to this plantation. All of the out-buildings, which made possible the mechanics of running the farm, were destroyed. With no money to rebuild the gin house, smoke house, stables, mills, etc., it was left in shambles, deteriorating rather rapidly. But one glance at it shows what a fine old house it had been in its glory days.

The Federals took everything from the house, then set the house on fire as they left. But faithful servants managed to put the fire out.

This is where Yankee soldiers put Harriet's wedding veil on a mule and rode off with it. After the Union Army left Cheraw, she returned here to find her old father with no coat on, in bitter cold weather. They took his coat. They took everything.

THE HOMESTEAD

In the photograph of the dilapidated house, the people shown are probably members of the Pollock family. After the war, Capt. A.A. Pollock bought The Homestead. Ada Evans Stevenson's aunt (sister of her mother from Salley, South Carolina) married Mr. Pollock. (Photo courtesy of Ada Evans Stevenson.)

Note:
When Harriet Powe married S.G. Godfrey during the war, her father, Thomas Ellerbe Powe, gave her his slave Solomon as a wedding gift. Solomon refused to leave her after the war, even though he was free to go. He lived out his life in a small house she had built for him. All of the older grandchildren remembered him when she lived at her home on Market Street. He was the beloved gardener, and was definitely part of the family. For all of their lives, they heard the story that Solomon had royal blood---that he was a prince in his African tribe.

Recently a new twist to the story has appeared. A biography of Dizzy Gillespie has come out. The title is *James Birks Gillespie*, by

Donald Maggen. The author went to Cheraw and interviewed some of Dizzy's relatives and friends, and went deeply into his genealogy. It seems that Thomas Ellerbe Powe went to Charleston and bought a slave girl who was an African princess, and he brought her back up to Cheraw. Tom Hyatt, who is descended from the Powes, did not know about this book, but he knew that Thomas Ellerbe Powe had fathered two children by her, and that this comes down in Dizzy's lineage. Dizzy, born John Birks Gillespie in Cheraw, claims he is descended from this royal princess.

My deduction is that Thomas Ellerbe Powe bought the two of them together---the slave girl <u>and</u> her brother Solomon, both claiming they had royal blood — that they were a prince and princess in their African tribe..

(Note)
After his wife Charlotte Harrington died, Thomas Ellerbe Powe never remarried.

Thomas Powe, brother of Harriet Powe Godfrey: killed at Gettysburg (From Adeline G. Merrill)

S.G. Godfrey was a First Lieutenant in the War Between the States. Mr. Malloy of Cheraw was a Captain. S.G. Godfrey was wounded in the leg at Gaines Mill---one of the seven days battles. His brother-in-law, Captain Thomas Powe, was killed, nearby at Gettysburg.

Great Uncle Thomas Powe was critically wounded and died very shortly afterwards in the Black Horse Tavern on the outskirts of the battlefield. This tavern was still standing when "Lep" and Will Godfrey, and Bill and Rob Thrower visited it while on a trip to the battlefields in 1934. After the war some of Uncle Tom's relatives, together with his servants and bodyguard, Wash Wingate, reclaimed his body. They brought it back to Cheraw and buried it in St. David's Cemetery in Cheraw.

From *All in One Southern Family, Volume II*

This is part of a letter from Bessie Powe Page to S.G. Godfrey II in Conway, S.C, dated 1949.

"I asked Emily if she could tell me who was sent to get Uncle Thomas Powe's body after the war. I also asked James. I reminded them that Wash Wingate, Uncle Thomas' bodyguard, was sent. They too remembered he was sent. Wash stayed with Uncle Thomas until he died, buried him—marking his grave. He was wounded July, 2, 1863 and died July 22, 1863. His personal belongings were brought back to Grandpa by Wash."

On the back of this letter is a note written by S.G. Godfrey II
(my father).

"Think Bessie mistaken as to Wash Wingate (colored) staying with Uncle Thomas until he died. Uncle Thomas was badly wounded and was taken to that house by my father, S.G. Godfrey and Wash. S.G. Godfrey was detailed by Captain Malloy to get Uncle Thomas off the field when he was wounded. Wash stayed at that house with Uncle T. until the Confederates had to retreat. The owner of the house was instructed by S.G.G. in the event Uncle T. died to bury him in the garden under a certain tree. After the war Wash probably was sent back to Gettysburg for the body.

S.G. Godfrey, Conway
March 5, 1949

END OF THE WAR

<u>Letters from John Evans:</u> U.S. Prison Johnson Island
(3 miles from Sandusky, Ohio May 12, 1865)

Dear Annie,

I have only time to drop a line to say I am well. I expected to send a letter by Lt. Leggett. He was expected to be released, as he applied to take the oath some time ago, but as yet he is here. Out of 2900 officers all have not applied except 60. I held out for a long time but when almost everybody left me I "caved in." I consider our cause as hopeless and the sooner we can get to our families to work for them the better. I don't know how those "Stay at home fighting men" will receive me. I believe tho' that Annie will welcome me and that is all I care about. There is no telling when we will be released. Everyone now seems to be waiting for Andy Jackson's Proclamation which is expected every day.

I have written you several letters. Only yours of March 13th received. Lep Godfrey is quite well and has been very kind to me, sharing his food and some supplies from home. Haile, Gibson, and Leggett---from Cheraw---are here. The others from Chesterfield here are Jim Craig, Moore, Sellers, and Courtney.

Johnson Island
Friday, June 16th, 1865

54

My dear wife,

As Lep Godfrey leaves today, I wish to say that I am getting along tolerably well all things considered. The time for my release seems to be coming on pretty rapidly. I was calculated to be discharged on Tuesday next. This will put me behind Godfrey about one week as I will stop in P. one day.

Tell my cute boy William he shall have a dog knife if one can be found. My anxiety for you all increases daily as I don't know how you are provided for food. Oh I hope that God has been merciful to you as well as he has been to me.

P.S.

David McIver goes with Lep, and Jas. S. Craig also goes with Lep.

THE LOST CAUSE MOVEMENT

It has been stated that the path Confederate women traveled to memorializing their military heroes culminated in the Lost Cause Movement. And that, thereafter, Sherman and the white women of the South were locked in an eternal war.

It is fascinating, and amusing as seen from the perspective of time, to unlock some of the stories of the Confederate women, and the roles they played after the Civil War.

I was of the third generation after the Civil war. I can remember teachers in the lower grades in Cheraw schools had large framed photographs of Stonewall Jackson and Robert E. Lee hung in the hallway outside their rooms. Miss Matt Duvall, first grade teacher, and Aunt Maggie Godfrey Thrower, second grade teacher, were the main ones that did this. They constantly told reverential stories to their students about Lee and Jackson and other heroes of that war.

In Grammar school we all marched into the auditorium for Chapel every day. Among other things on the agenda there was a lot of singing from The Golden Book of Favorite Songs.

Quote from Jennie Llew Finlayson (Mrs. Clarence Guyton—of Columbia):

"When I was about 11 years old, Miss Gumm (music teacher) was late coming to Chapel, so Mr. McCown asked me if I could play something for everyone to march to, when coming into the auditorium. So I pranced up to the piano (he really was desperate!) and began The Battle Hymn of the Republic, one of my favorites! Well, Miss Matt Duvall and Mrs. Thrower came over to the piano bench and carefully slid me off, whispering softly, 'Oh no, honey, don't ever play that again!' I thought I had committed the <u>unpardonable</u> sin until I looked to the right and saw Miss Gumm standing in the doorway smiling, and Mr. McCown smiling, too. Miss Gumm said, 'That's all right, Jennie Llew, I'll play now---and Mr. McCown told me I could go right back to my seat. I wouldn't tell Mother, for I was afraid to, thinking I'd done something <u>awful!</u> Well, I don't blame Miss Matt and Mrs. Thrower since they, like our grandmother, were young girls during the Civil War, and I'm sure they hated <u>anything</u> yankee-ish."

<u>Other examples of typical reactions of the women in the South:</u>

Northerners were bitterly resented. Lucille Godfrey's Aunt Ellen Cooper (*from Conway*) married Charles Johnson, a Northerner. Even though he fought with the Confederates, <u>and lost a leg,</u> his mother-in-law never accepted him. She would only refer to him as "Mr. Johnson," or merely "Johnson"!

Martha Derrick told of a man in Orangeburg who bought a Lincoln. His wife made him take it back!

Postscript

I have no data to confirm my convictions. I have nothing about other towns and cities in other states. But Cheraw gets my vote as the "Epicenter of the Lost Cause Movement."

Case in Point: My grandmother, Harriet Powe Godfrey, would not allow Sherman's name to be spoken in her house, nor any American flag to be flown on her property. She would not even let the mailman deliver her mail because he wore a blue uniform and worked for the Government!

Her son worked downtown near the post office, so he stopped by every day to pick up her mail and bring it to her.

Adeline Godfrey Pringle Merrill
March 2009

The Burial of Latane

As a child I remember standing in Uncle Rob and Aunt Bet Godfrey's parlor and gazing up at a framed print: The Burial of Latane. It had a peculiar if not morbid fascination for me. Possibly I might have been drawn to it because of the aura, pathos, and reverence it seemed to generate among the older generation. Recently I have come across the book *The Confederate Image – Prints of the Lost Cause.* So beautifully did it explain the grip and spell that this print held over the people of the South that I decided to include a portion of the introduction here.

THE BURIAL OF LATANE

A.G. Campbell, after William D. Washington. Signed lower left: W.D. Washington 1864. Among the most popular of all prints of the Lost Cause, Campbell's engraving was a tribute to the sacrifices of the heroic women of the Confederacy.

Taken from the introduction of the book *The Confederate Image - Prints of the Lost Cause*

THE BURIAL OF LATANE

Douglas Southall Freeman, eminent historian of the Confederacy and biographer of Robert E. Lee, remembered Southern children "gazing from infancy" at an inspiring picture that graced the walls of many of their homes. By questioning their mothers and fathers about these pictures, Freeman recalled, new generations of Southerners had learned "with their first history lessons the story that inspired their parents." Frank Vandiver spoke of its "fantastic popularity," saying, "Copies can still be found in attics and other hiding places." And as late as 1976, Virginius Dabney reported that the picture "still hangs in Richmond homes."

The ubiquitous picture of which these scholars spoke was a nineteenth-century engraving showing a group of white women and black slaves performing a burial service over a coffin draped with a heavy cavalry overcoat. Not only was it a representative tribute to the Southern dead but it also depicted "the spirit of the women of the South." It touched a special chord of memory for the people of the South. The Virginia Judge who purchased the original on which the engraving was based testified that he had heard the story of the picture "since I was a child, and throughout my life have seen many of the steel engravings hanging on walls of this county and neighboring counties. I really believe that these engravings helped to hold the Southern People together as one after the war."

The engraving was entitled The Burial of Latane, and its story originated in the Peninsular Campaign of 1862 when the Confederacy repulsed the first massive assault against Richmond. The new heroes who emerged after this victory captured the popular imagination. Chief among them was Robert E. Lee and J.E.B. ("Jeb") Stuart, who staged a dramatic and daring four-day reconnaissance ride around the entire Union force, providing Lee with information crucial to Confederate success. Stuart lost only one man during the entire mission -- a twenty-nine year old doctor named William D. Latane. This lone casualty, a captain of volunteers from a prominent Virginia family, would come to enjoy a fame that for a time rivaled that of his daring commander.

Stuart had ordered the company nearest the enemy to attack. It was Latane's unit. Captain Latane - who charged ahead, sword drawn, in a failed attempt to behead the rival commander - was shot four or five times and killed. Latane's violent death ignited an instant legend.

Not even Jeb Stuart could have predicted that Latane would become more than an inspiration to a small unit of troops -- that instead, he would be transformed into one of the best-known and most deeply mourned of all the lower-echelon casualties of the war.

The sanctification was attributable to a poem and, in large measure, to a popular print. The print did not, however, portray Latane's charge or fall, but, rather, the way he was laid to rest. An original artistic response to a commonplace occurrence of war successfully elevated this minor tragedy into a major legend.

After Latane's death, his brother John, a lieutenant in the same company, took charge of the body. When a corn cart from the nearby Westwood Plantation rolled into view, John Latane asked whether it might be used to transport his brother's remains away from the fighting. Aided by the slave who was driving the wagon, Latane cleared the cart of its cargo, loaded his dead brother into the back, and returned with the body to Westwood, two miles away.

There were no white men living there at the time -- all were at the front -- but Mrs. William Brockenbrough, the mistress of Westwood, took the body into her home and sent Lieutenant Latane back to his unit, assuring him that William would be buried "as tenderly as if he were her brother." A neighbor observed, "Oh, what a sad office. This dear young soldier, so precious too many hearts, now in the hands of sorrowing, sympathizing friends, yet, personally, strangers, to him." She did not know it but it turns out that she was touching on a cultural nerve. So many young Southern soldiers were dying alone in unfamiliar places that the Latane episode could symbolize the collective fears and hopes of the entire Confederacy. These women became the symbolic angels of mercy prayed for by every mother whose son might face a similar fate.

The day after the battle, slaves from Westwood and Summer Hill fashioned a simple coffin and cleaned and dressed the body. Mrs. Brockenbrough cut a lock from Latane's hair, "as the only thing we could do for his mother." Then she dispatched a slave to fetch the family minister to preach the funeral service. But Union pickets blocked the messenger, preventing him from reaching the clergymen.

And so the women "took the body of our poor young Captain, and buried it ourselves in the graveyard at Summer Hill, with no one to interrupt us." Mrs. Newton, neighbor, read the Episcopal funeral service herself, witnessed by Mrs. Brockenbrough, a few slaves, and a group of small children; the little girls covered "his honored grave with flowers." Latane and a member of the plantation family killed earlier in the war now lay "side by side," Mrs. Newton recalled, "martyrs to a holy cause."

Almost immediately, the details of Latane's death and burial were widely reported in the Richmond newspapers. Then John R. Thompson contributed a eulogy in verse. He served the cause with poetic tributes to Confederate martyrs, including Turner Ashby and Jeb Stuart. The most famous of his efforts described the death and burial of the captain from Virginia, a tribute not only to "our early lost, lamented LATANE," but to the heroic women who had laid his body to rest. It was these women who

.. in accents soft and low,
Trembling with pity, touched with pathos, read
Over his hallowed dust the ritual for the dead.

One of the Virginians who undoubtedly read or heard recitations of Thompson's poem was a young local artist named <u>William DeHarburn Washington</u>, a distant relative of the first president. Washington had studied art under Emanuel Leutz. Well-schooled in historical painting, the Confederate artist decided to attempt what he probably supposed would be a highly saleable canvas based on <u>"The Burial of Latane"</u>. Mrs. Newton, with prayer book in hand, was to be the central figure of the scene.

Washington completed his 4' by 3' canvas (plate 1) in 1864. It was exhibited in several places and reportedly attracted "Throngs of visitors" and created "a furor." It then was exhibited at the Virginia State Capitol where a bucket was placed in front of it to encourage donations to the cause. A bit of folklore claims that a farm woman sold her cow to come all the way to Richmond so she could throw her wedding ring into the collection pail."

The engraving was produced by A.G. Campbell, who worked from a photograph of Washington's canvas. The print sold at first for twenty dollars, a hefty sum in the impoverished postwar South, and its broad circulation testifies to the devotion the Lost Cause would inspire for years to come.

Campbell's print of <u>The Burial of Latane</u> became one of the most famous icons of the Lost Cause, a tribute to the vision of its artist, the skill of its engraver, and the marketing ingenuity of its publisher and promoters. By capturing both the universal sorrow over so many young men lost in war and the valor of Southern women left behind to raise families, maintain homes, and cope with emergencies, the picture registered an emotional impact on several levels. It extolled the virtues of womanhood and faith and the common bond of mass mourning, and, not incidentally, it portrayed black men as eternally loyal to the peculiar institution that shackled them. The comfortable mixing of black and white people, suggesting harmonious master/slave relations, must have appealed to whites who felt threatened by sweeping changes in the South's racial system after the war. Writing in the *Confederate Veteran*, Mrs. William Lyne recognized that above all, the print symbolized "the sacredness of those days when the women of the South had to take the place of men and even read the burial service for the dead, for the men were all in the war." Douglas Southall Freeman thought it uniquely expressive of a "tradition of the lofty devotion of womanhood."

SCENES OF HISTORIC SITES
IN AND NEAR CHERAW

INTERIOR OF OLD
ST. DAVID

STAIN GLASS FROM
ST. DAVID

TOWN HALL
IRON STEPS AND
GRILLWORK BY
CHRISTOPHER
WERNER,
CELEBRATED
IRONWORKER OF
CHARLESTON, SC

BUILT BY WILLIAM C. ELLERBE
(BROTHER OF ESTHER ELLERBE)
GENERAL LAFAYETTE WAS ENTERTAINED IN THIS HOUSE IN 1825
CHERAW WAS DESCRIBED BY A 19TH CENTURY HISTORIAN AS
"THE PRETTIEST TOWN IN DIXIE."

The Merchants Bank of South Carolina

THE MERCHANTS BANK OF SOUTH CAROLINIA - CHERAW, SOUTH CAROLINIA

The largest bank in South Carolina prior to the Confederate War, and the last bank in the South to honor Confederate money. It also was one of the last banks in the Confederacy to suspend special payments during the war.

Built in 1835, the building is of brick construction, colonial style, and was designed by Peter Conlaw Lynch, father of Bishop Lynch, Roman Catholic Bishop of South Carolina, and prominent in the Confederacy. A Mr. Dunlap was associated with Mr. Lynch in promoting a brickyard and in making the brick used for this building.

William Godfrey *(Great-grandfather of Adeline Godfrey Merrill)* started as a cashier here, living in the upper quarters with his family, as was the custom for the job--which mainly was to protect the safe. He eventually became President of this bank.

Quote from an article in *The Cheraw Chronicle* titled "Oldest buildings in Cheraw" (1933)

"The Merchants Bank did the banking for several North Carolina as well as South Carolina counties. It was the financial office of the Confederacy in this section, and when the Confederate Army retreated from Cheraw on March 3rd, 1865, as Sherman entered the town, Gen. Hardee, in command of the Confederate forces, drew out $67,000, the balance that was on the book for the Confederacy. The bank never recovered from the effects of the war, and closed early in the summer of 1865."

NEW MATERIAL AS TO THE ROLE THIS BANK PLAYED IN THE CONFEDERATE WAR HAS JUST RECENTLY BEEN PROVIDED BY HENRY P. BOYD, CHATTANOOGA, TN - TO ADELINE G. MERRILL

August 22, 2009

Dear Adeline,

Enclosed you will find a sample proof of the page for William Godfrey as it will appear in George Premmel's publication. I have enclosed a copy of a CS Treasury IDR signed by Godfrey, and a brief explanation of the purpose of a CS Treasury IDR (Interim Deposit Receipt). Also enclosed are some copies of Bank Notes issued by the Merchants Bank of Cheraw SC that William Godfrey signed.

As you probably know, banks printed and issued their own currency prior to the establishment of a national currency system in the early 1900's.

Let me take this opportunity to thank you for your help in obtaining an image of Godfrey, and your prompt attention transmitting it.

Information from George Premmel, a Student of the Confederate Treasury Dept., and collector of Confederate bills:

IDRs were used to record the fact that an individual deposited CSA treasury notes at a depository office. This was usually done for the purchase of new Treasury bonds or to exchange old currency (about to be recalled) for new Treasury notes. Often the demand for new bonds and notes exceeded the CSA Treasury printers' ability to produce them. These certificates were to be held until the new bonds and notes were available and then exchanged for them.

They were not bearer bonds nor substitute currency. That said, the named owner of an IDR could assign ownership to another with the appropriate notation and signature on the back. This was usually done to pay taxes and the IDR was assigned to a tax collector.

IDRs were issued in many cities and towns in all eleven Confederate states. They were even issued by CS army quartermaster and payroll officers to troops in the field. The certificates were all signed by a depositary or his deputy and the locations were printed or written in. A large part of the new book is an illustrated catalog of IDRs by state and town.

William R. Godfrey (1802-85) President Merchants Bank of South Carolina
and Depositary of the Cheraw SC Depository Office

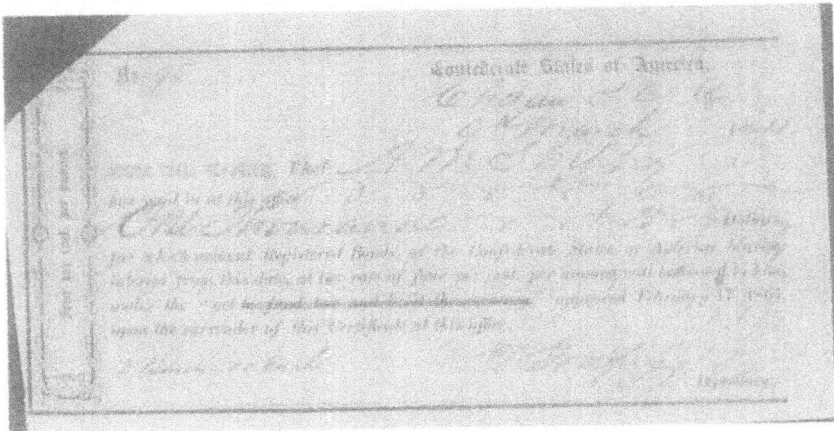

IDR (SC-55) Signed by William R. Godfrey

ADELINE GODFREY MERRILL

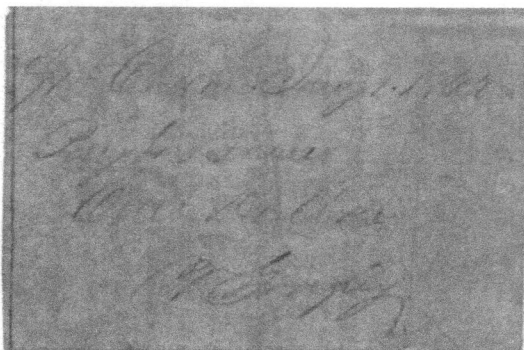

<u>From notes taken during a telephone conversation with Mr.</u>
<u>Henry Boyd, 8/19/09</u> *(Adeline Godfrey Merrill)*

"The Treasury Dept. of the Confederacy appointed William Godfrey, <u>Treasury Agent.</u> His job was to handle the Confederate money in that area and parts of North Carolina. He also had a branch office at Mars Bluff. If there was any counterfeit money, that would be recalled. Bonds were refinarced. The way the Confederate financing system was run had to be "creative" because the whole thing was running on credit. The value of currency depreciated."

"All the money was printed in Columbia. When Sherman came to South Carolina the Litho Stones (for the printing presses) were moved for safety. More money got printed after the war. All banks issued currency. There was no cash to exchange."

**

There is an additional story in this Bank's history, told in the same <u>Cheraw Chronicle</u> article mentioned earlier: <u>Oldest Buildings in Cheraw</u> (1933) *(This has nothing to do with the Civil War, but it is a marvelous little story.)*

"In 1852, the Bank sent $5000 in currency by registered mail to a bank in Natchez, Miss. The package never reached the destination. The Post Office authorities in investigating it found that it reached Atlanta but could not find where it left there. The postal inspector, in checking over the books in the Atlanta post office, saw that the registry book for the day that the package reached there, was in a different handwriting than that of the postmaster, and of his one clerk. On asking who wrote up the book that day, the postmaster told him that a young man who clerked in a store came in sometimes, and helped them. The clerk was arrested and in his trunk was found $4200. He admitted that he had taken the money."

"This young man was very much interested in music. Jennie Lind, the famous singer who came from Europe to sing in New York, went to Charleston (then the center of culture of the South) and gave a few concerts. This young man had taken a party of eighteen young people to Charleston to hear Jenny Lind. That was what he had used the missing $800 for."

**

Cody Godfrey wrote that during the Depression people living on Market Street in Cheraw started renting rooms to tourists on their way to and from Florida. Highway I came right through the middle of the town on Market Street. This was before the days of motels along the highways. By opening their homes for tourists, this was the only way for some homes to take in a little money.

During the Depression Mrs. Henry Harrall restored <u>The Old Merchants Bank</u> and made it into a Tourist Bed & Breakfast. It was named <u>The Cherokee Inn.</u> But it has long since been converted back to its original use - a bank.

Cheraw Lyceum Building eracted in early 1820's and used by General Sherman an office during the period of occupancy of Cheraw by the Union Soldiers.

The Town Hall. Had an upstairs used for Balls, Dances and other gatherings. Before radio, Mr. Will Godfrey *(Grandson of William Godfrey, the banker)* participated in the World Series of Baseball here at the Town Hall. Each pitch and play came in by telegraph. A large board with a drawing of the diamond was set up, with the name of base runners in position. He knew telegraphy and usually called the plays.

Lafayette House built in 1823, this house has entrances on all four sides and his named after General Lafayette after his 1825 visit where a public reception and ball was given in his honor.

The covered bridge was still part of the bridge in my day in the 1920's and 1930's to cross the Pee Dee River. When riding over this bridge I used to study the floor planks fearfully, and looked at the water below through spaces in the side of the Covered Bridge – Adeline Godfrey Merrill

In 1909 the steel bridge replaced the most of the Cover Bridge over the Pee Dee River after the flood of 1908.

Pee Dee River Bridge
Cheraw, S. C.

THE OLD COVERED BRIDGE - CHERAW, SOUTH CAROLINIA

OLD TOWN BRIDGE ACROSS PEE DEE CHERAW S

From *All In One Southern Family, Volume II*
by Adeline G. Merrill "Queen" Godfrey Wilson's
memories of the <u>Old Bridge</u> -

"I used to ride in a buggy over the old covered bridge with Aunt
Maggie Thrower. The red hill was steep, down to the narrow approach to the bridge. I think I remember the small Toll House on the
left. Inside the bridge it was dim and dusty and smelled of horse ma-
nure. Spaced along were diamond shaped windows you could see out,
whether on land or over water. When I knew we were over the river
itself I literally held my breath in fright. The bridge had a curve in it

77

and arriving safely on firm ground my fears were only partially re-
lieved because the road took an abrupt turn to the right and followed
alongside the river for awhile: Tales were told about the bridge - --it
was said that some people who crossed it in the <u>dark,</u> said a ghostly
hand would touch the horse and bring him to a dead stop-- till he
raced on in fright."

"In the big flood of August 1908, most of the Covered Bridge was
washed away. Later a new open bridge was attached to the portion
of the Covered Bridge that was left -- and even later it all was destroyed, as that road was discontinued. A new bridge was built farther up the river. But for a good while before that first bridge was
fixed, our only way to cross the river was by ferry. I <u>hated</u> crossing it
because the river bank on the Marlboro side was slick and steep and
sometimes Dad's car would slip back on to the ferry, which wobbled
and wouldn't stay steady."

The Iron Bridge, Cheraw, S. C.

PHOTOS OF BRIDGES COURTESY OF MARSHALL & SUSAN MCMILLAN

"Yesterday evening the many friends of Miss Ida Stogner and Mr. M.C. Thomas were taken by surprise when the announcement was made that they had been married. The ceremony was performed under rather romantic circumstances. The bridal party, accompanied by a few friends and the officiating minister, Rev. A.H. McArn, riding in automobiles, stopped on the bridge crossing the Pee Dee River at about 8 o'clock. There they were — mad man and wife."
The Cheraw Daily Herald, June 29, 1911

PEE DEE RIVER BRIDGE, 600 FT. IN LENGTH—JEFFERSON DAVIS HIGHWAY—CHERAW, S. C.

STEEL BRIDGE

Cheraw's steel bridge was constructed in 1908-1909 to replace the old wooden bridge that was washed away in August 1908. A short portion of the wooden bridge that remained served as the entrance to the steel bridge on the Cheraw side. This 600 foot steel structure remained in use for 30 years until the present bridge was constructed further upstream. It was opened for use in 1939, and the steel bridge was torn down a short time later.

THE TEACHERAGE

(From article in the Chesterfield Shopper, Cheraw, SOUTH CAROLINIA Volume IV, No. 42 March, 1986 by Lynn Ingram Laney

THE TEACHERAGE - REAR VIEW **320 3RD ST**
CHERAW, SC OLDEST HOUSE IN CHERAW

Date: Possibly as early as 1780

Duncan & Mary Ann Malloy were the first family known to have occupied it. All six of their children served in the Civil War. One son, Theodore, was Capt. of Company C in the 8th Regiment, being given that position after Capt. Thomas E. Powe was killed at Gettysburg. Margaret Malloy Duvall and husband, Howard, bought it in 1913. It was used as a rental property until 1941, when it was sold to Margaret Manning Malloy. She continued to rent it as a duplex. Many of the renters from the 1930's on were teachers, and this is where the house got its name.

THE TEACHERAGE - FRONT VIEW
HOME OF MR. & MRS. JAMES A. SPRUILL III

Margaret Manning Malloy's son, Manning Malloy, inherited both the Teacherage and the Lafayette House in 1973. In 1978, he sold the residence to James A. Spruill III and Sarah C. Spruill. The deed included a preservation covenant that no alterations or changes could be undertaken without written approval of the Chesterfield County Preservation Commission. Also, to be protected, were six magnolia trees, planted in honor of Mary Ann Malloy's six sons who served in the Civil War.

Copy of letter from Jim Spruill, Cheraw, SC 8/6/2009

Dear Ad,

I have enjoyed your stories about Cheraw with Sherman and his folks. Mother *(Eleanor Duvall Spruill, watercolor artist)* used to tell an additional one which I thought was lovely.

Her grandfather, Mr. H.P. Duvall, was 18 when Sherman got here. He had not been in the army but, as a member of the home guard, he went out to meet Sherman's army in the fortification they had built on Thompson Creek south of town.

When Mother was a little girl she sat on her grandfather's knee and he would say, "Do you know what I did when I saw the Yankees coming, Tootsie?" She would answer, "No, Grandfather, what did you do?" His reply was, "I ran, Tootsie, I ran." And he had run all the way home.

Sarah has said she would send this letter with the picture you requested. Hope you enjoy it.

With best regards -

Jim Spruill

Photo courtesy of Peyre Pringle

HOME OF ELEANOR & E. WALKER DUVALL
(PARENTS OF ELEANOR DUVALL SPRUILL)

THE HARTZELL HOUSE - BUILT BY ERASMUS POWE
1790

(Information from Ronald Ellerbe's list of famous houses in Cheraw)

Eramus Powe had this house built as a wedding gift for his daughter Elizabeth, who married James Robert Ervin (Sen. Sam Ervin's ancestor.)

In 1850, the house was acquired by Henry McIver - whose wife was the granddaughter of Gen. Erasmus Powe. Henry McIver was for many years, the Chief Justice of the Supreme Court of South Carolina. The large side wing, *(not shown here)* was once the law firm of Chief Justice Henry McIver and was moved here from town.

When Sherman's army arrived in Cheraw on March 3, 1865, Gen. Sherman selected this house as his personal headquarters. Henry McIver was away at the time, being a Captain in Wade Hampton's Cavalry. Mrs. McIver said she and her children moved upstairs while General Sherman occupied the lower floor. She always said that Sherman treated her with the greatest courtesy and had the children come down and eat with him. She was thankful because the family had no food.

His law partner, John A. Inglis, was the main author of the South Carolina Ordinance of Secession and Sherman had issued a $10,000 reward for the arrest of Judge Inglis.

BOXWOOD HALL

Dr. Thomas Ellerbe Powe purchased "Boxwood Hall" (formerly called "Heartsease") in 1822. It is a gracious two-story Williamsburg style house. When he married Charlotte Harrinngton in 1822, he brought his bride home to Boxwood Hall.

All of their children were born here, including two Daughters who figure in this story:

Caroline, who married Judge McIver --
(Grandmother of Helen Wanamaker)
Harriet, who married SG Godfrey --
(Grandmother of Adeline Godfrey)

When Sherman's army was approaching Cheraw, family members hid a supply of bacon underneath the floor boards of a second story bedroom. This left a greasy spot on the ceiling of the parlor room below, which seemed to show, no matter how many times it was painted over. The late Jean Harris, former owner, said that that spot was still a problem when she lived there, before the recent owners bought the house.

As a pre-teenager I spent many a night here with my friend and cousin, Helen Wannamaker, and we were fascinated with the story of the "greasy spot" caused by the bacon. Boxwood Hall was s second home for me. It was in that extra-large hall, with an informal sitting room created in the back, that I heard my first radio. What a marvel! I wish I had a recording of Helen trying to explain how it worked!

When Sherman's troops shelled the town in 1865, a cannonball struck the floor on the front porch and cut part of the railing. That mark could still be seen, and also the ball that struck and did the damage.

(Adeline Godfrey Merrill)

(**PHOTO TAKEN FROM THE 2000 CHERAW CALENDAR BOOKLET**)

ENFIELD

This was the headquarters for Union Gen. W.T. Sherman's second in command, Gen. Oliver Howard, during the Confederate War.

Enfield was built by Erasmus Powe as a wedding gift for his daughter Martha, who married John Ellerbe. He also planted the row of cedars in front of the house.

This house suffered from the Charleston earthquake in 1886, and a major fire. At the time of this photo, Enfield was the residence of long time 20th century owners John and Caroline Nock.

420 CHURCH STREET

This shows the house as it is today. There is an unusual feature for the architecture of the porch. The idea of an indented porch, with roof supported by freestanding columns to the ground (the columns resting on pillars or stoops) came from the Barbados to Charleston, and then up the Pee Dee region.

Quote from *Cheraw Chronicle* (1927): "This fine old residence was erected in 1825. The Misses Eliza and Margaret Ellerbe bought it in 1845. After Miss Eliza died, Margaret Ellerbe married John H. McIver, who for over 40 years was treasurer of the Cheraw and Darlington - and the Cheraw and Salisbury Railroads, both roads eventually being a part of the Atlantic Coast Line system.

The first Japonicas brought to Cheraw were planted by Margaret McIver and the finest specimen of boxwood in Cheraw is on the large front lawn. The Japinicas were brought from Charleston.

Mrs. S.G. Goldfrey II purchased it in 1916.

Built in 1825, the home of Dr. and Mrs. James Leppard, Jr., is located at 420 Church Street in Cheraw. Photo by Phil Powell, courtesy of Sarah Spruill.

420 Church Street is the birthplace of Lucille, Adeline, and Eleanor Godfrey. (Oldest sister, Esther, was born in a house on Market Street.) All were raised here.

At right: *This photograph is out of focus, but it shows the tremendous boxwood (now gone) and the gigantic magnolia tree.*

Precious little library in Society Hill – about 12 miles from Cheraw.

The one-room Society Hill library building shown here, houses rare old volumes. A library society was established in this small town in 1822, and is still a live organization. Offers for the book collection, from the Carnegie Institution have been refused. Source: 1856 article.

CONDENSED FROM ARTICLE IN CHERAW CHRONICLE 1856 BY GENEVIEVE REYNOLDS

"A little one room, wooden Society Hill building, fifteen feet by twenty, and its contents are estimated to be worth more than ten thousand dollars in cash money, and two million or more dollars in sentiment. *(Written in 1856)*

No one lives there but it is visited by scores of people who come from all parts of the country to see the picturesque village of Society Hill and its treasures.

This quaint small structure has a fireplace extending seven feet across half of one side of the one room which furnishes heat for the building.

No library of that period would have been complete without copies of Greek, Latin, French, and German classics and especially Greek and Latin, all the writings of Cicero, Vergil, Plautus, Livy, Goethe, Homer, and Terence. Of course, Rabelais, Daudet, and Moliere have their niche on the shelves along with their brothers and sisters of the fine arts. One may see several copies of The Iliad, The Odyssey, Faust, and Dante's Inferno.

Scott, Dickens, and Sims provide most of the fiction for the readers of the early eighteen hundreds. Poetry had little or no place in the collection.

Thomas Smith, M.D. purchased the books ... & established a library for residents within a five-mile radius. Memberships were fixed at $20.

A resolution was passed so that "persons not members of the society residing in the village of Society Hill or not farther distance than five miles from the village, may with the consent of the librarian and purchasing committee have the use of the books upon payment of five dollars per year. Such persons using books by annual payment of five dollars, shall forfeit their privilege of taking out books, should they remove farther than five miles from Society Hill."

This Article appeared in the April 1970, _Sandlapper_ on the occasion of celebrating South Carolinian's Tri-centennial. At that time the Pegues House was 200 years old. Now, in 2009, Marlboro County seat - Bennettsville, is almost 190 years old, and the Pegues place, the county's oldest existing house, has become almost 240 year old. It was built in 1770.

Pegues Place   By Margaret P. (Pegues) Kinney   April 1970, _The Sandlapper_

Map Showing Pegues House Location

About one mile east of Pee Dee River, just below the North Carolina
boundary and one mile West of U.S. 1

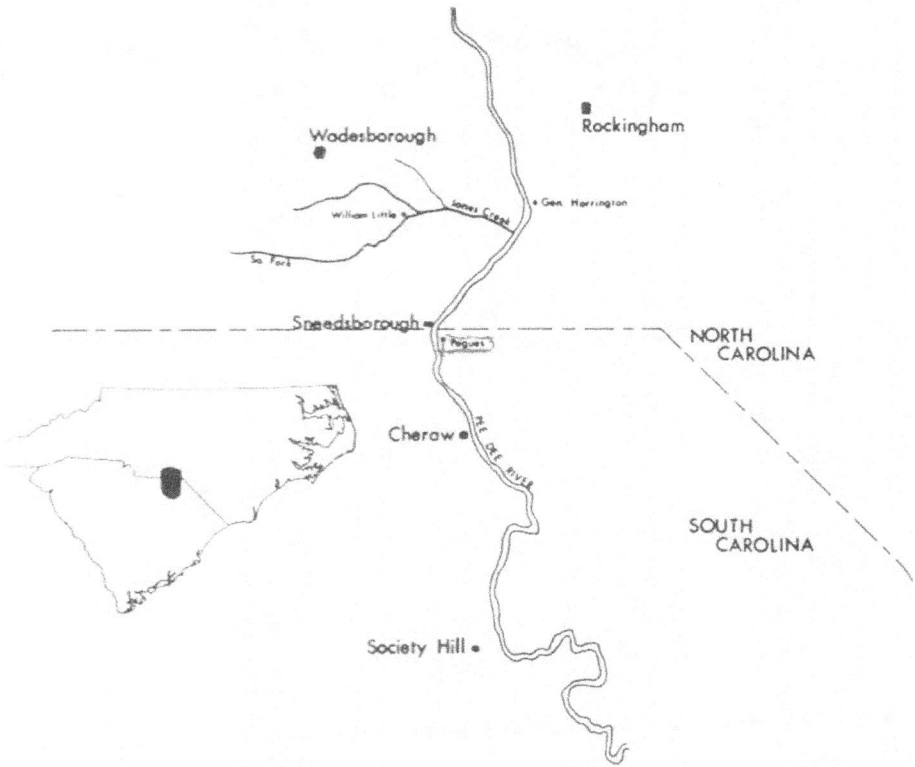

PEGUES HOUSE

From Cheraw Chronicle article: <u>Commissioned to Paint F.B.P. Pegues House</u> (1930?)

"Wofford Finlayson, Cheraw's artist, who has just completed a canvas in oil of St. David's Church for the Public Works of Art project, has been commissioned to make a like painting of the old Claudius Pegues home, better known to our citizens today as the Frank Brooks Pegues house, which is located nine miles north of Cheraw on Highway 1."

"This old home was erected before the Revolution by Claudius Pegues, who later was a Colonel in General Harrington's Brigade, which did eminent service in the War of the Revolution. The home since it was built has been in continuous possession of the Pegues family and has a unique history."

From *All In One Southern Family, Volume 1,* by Adeline G. Merrill

"In the Revolution, the British had repeatedly refused to exchange prisoners with the Americans. Finally, in the summer of 1780, after the Battle of Guilford Court House and after Nathaniel Greene had returned to Camden, Cornwallis had reached Wilmington, North Carolina with the British army. The negotiations for exchange of prisoners were again resumed. This resulted in Lord Cornwallis sending Captain Cornwallis, a cousin, to meet Gen. Harrington (*grandfather of Charlotte*), who had been named by Nathaniel Greene to draw up a Cartel of agreement. The place for the meeting of these officers was the Claudius Pegues home, which was approximately halfway between the two armies. There the agreement was made - the only one during the War of the Revolution."

"As a result of this meeting, thousands of prisoners were exchanged, among them the British general Burgoyne - who had been captured at the Battle of Saratoga some two years before. He was exchanged with General Moultrie, who had been captured by the British at the Siege of Charleston the previous year."

"In a few months after this exchange the war terminated by Cornwallis surrendering to Washington at Yorktown."

The following information on the Pegues House is taken from an article which appeared in *The Sandlapper* in April, 1970, by Margaret Pegues Kinney

"Claudius Pegues, with his wife and two sons, left his mercantile business in Georgetown about 1760, and moved inland to the sparsely settled area of colonial Craven County known as the Cheraws.

Now more than 200 years later, his descendants celebrate his courage in coming to this place and building in 1770, for himself and generations to follow a stately country home and a legacy of good deeds."

"Masters of the plantation once controlled as much as 20,000 acres of rich river soil on both sides of the Pee Dee, from near Cheraw to well into North Carolina territory. Today fifth and sixth generation descendants own some 5,000 acres of this land granted to Claudius Pegues by the English Kings George II and III."

"In the home's 200 years, occupants have always been Pegueses. Living there since 1958, have been Mr. & Mrs. Paul Fitzsimmons Hammond -- she being the former Jennie May Pegues. Prior to this, it was the home of her brothers, the late Victor Rene Pegues and Preston Brooks Pegues."

"The first Claudius Pegues became a prosperous and respected man after his emigration at age 16 to Charles-Town in 1736. As French Huguenots, his parents had fled France after the revocation of the Edict of Nantes and settled in London. The young Pegues was born in England in 1719, but sought his fame and fortune in the New World. A plaque in the old Huguenot Church in Charleston bears his name and witnesses his success. In Georgetown, he was a member of the Winyah Indigo Society and Prince George Parish, Winyah."

"His Pee Dee home is of unusual architectural excellence for a home of that era located in an uncultured environment 175 miles from the city of Charles Towne."

"Some of the 18th-century Low-country and English furnishings are still used and treasured by the Pegues descendants in the home."

"Old family portraits also adorn the dining room. One is of a Pegues cousin, <u>Wilson Godfrey</u> of Cheraw, who was master of ceremonies at the ball honoring the Marquis de Lafayette when he visited here on his triumphant tour of the United States in 1825. Another is Godfrey's sister, <u>Harriet Godfrey Gillespie,</u> great-grandmother of Jennie May Pegues Hammond."*

"Because its masters were such active and able Whigs, the mansion seems to have been a favored meeting place. The only exchange of prisoners actually completed in the United States between Continental and British armies was agreed upon at the Claudius Pegues house on May 3, 1781."

"Frequent visitors at the home were generals Greene and 'Light Horse Harry' Lee, father of Gen. Robert E. Lee."

"Cotton was raised on the rich soil. But soon to follow were the dark days of The War Between the States, when again war would visit this historic house."

"Gen. Sherman's Union forces, after burning Columbia, came north from Cheraw and encamped in the large field in front of the home place, en route to Rockingham, North Carolina. Enlisted men tried to burn the house but officers billeted there put the fire out, according to family history. The aged widow of James Pegues died just five days after the plantation was ravaged. (The Yankees had destroyed her medicines, it is said.) A 10-foot grandfather clock which once stood in the dining room was defaced by the saber of an irate Yankee soldier. A union cannon ball which has rested for years under a giant magnolia in the front yard of the home provides a reminder of those days of unrest."

Footnote

My apologies to the disinterested reader who cares not for the genealogy of others. But the younger generations in my family need to understand this startling fact about the origin of the name Samuel Gillespie Godfrey.

Harriet Godfrey, sister of William Godfrey, married Mr. Samuel Gillespie. In other words, William Godfrey named his first son for his brother-in-law! This is where the name Samuel Gillespie Godfrey originated. Our only relation to the Gillespie family is that my great-aunt married a Gillespie.

I have fond memories of Sunday drives out to Pegues House and visiting with these cousins. Note: As of December 2009 this old house has fallen into a sad state of neglect and disrepair.

ADDENDUM

SUMMARY OF THOMAS POWE, ERASMUS POWE,

AND THOMAS ELLERBE POWE

AND THE HOUSES THEY BUILT

EARLY HISTORY - FIRST SETTLERS

THE HOUSES OF

THOMAS POWE - ERASMUS POWE - THOMAS EL- LERBE POWE

I. THOMAS POWE

This is the Thomas Powe who heads our cherished family tree: The Line of Descent of Thomas Powe, compiled by William Godfrey, 1931, and revised and executed by Rob Thrower, in 1936.

The following information is taken from the Cheraw Chronicle article (1933), Some of Cheraw's Oldest Buildings

"The oldest house in this section is the old Thomas Powe house, five miles north of town on the Wadesboro road, now owned by R.K. Laney."

"Thomas Powe first settled in the village of Society Hill, but later built this house at Orange Hill in 1765. He was one of the officers of St. David's Church when old St. David's was built. When the first Legislature of South Carolina met after the war of the Revolution in 1785, he was appointed on a commission to divide Cheraw district into three counties, and to name and locate the county seats. The result of this commission's work was Chesterfield, Marlboro, and Darlington Counties, and at that time Darlington covered a large part of what is now Florence County. The commission named Chesterfield, Bennettsville, and Darlington as county seats."

"This house, built in 1765, still stands in its original form today (1933)."

Note

The house was torn down in the 1940's. The lumber inside was used in Mr. Coggershell's new home being built, and some of the

lumber was used in the house named <u>Enfield</u> (built by Thomas Powe's son, Erasmus Powe) when that house was being restored after a fire.

Thomas Powe was married three times:

> *1st wife - Mary Chapman*
> *2nd wife - Rachel Allen (our ancestor)*
> *3rd wife - Rebecca Ford Spencer (widow of Calvin Spencer -- and ancestor of my daughter-in-law Mary Baker Pringle!)*

(There is a rather dramatic ending to all this when we get to the matter of Thomas Powe's will.)

Quoted from <u>All In One Southern Family, Volume 1</u> (AGM)
"Thomas Powe was honored by his contemporaries with many public trusts (*History of Old Cheraws*). He was clerk of the circuit Court of General Sessions and Common Pleas for Cheraw District in 1778, and held that same office when in 1779, seven Tories were convicted of sedition. The records recite that six were hung and the seventh had his right ear cut off, and was whipped. (S.S. Historical Commission, Columbia, South Carolina) Thomas Powe was chosen a member of the House for St. David's Parish in the Legislature in 1784-85. He was re-elected in 1790 as representative from Chesterfield Co. He was a charter member of the famous St. David's Society, and held many offices too numerous to mention. He served as vestryman and warden in St. David's Church in Cheraw for many years. Truly his descendants have a great heritage in the life of Thomas Powe and should pattern their lives from this Famous ancestor."

II. <u>ERASMUS POWE</u>

<u>The Homestead</u> was built by Gen. Erasmus Powe about 1806. He built this house very close to the house of his father, Thomas Powe - out on the Wadesboro road 5 miles from town.

It should be noted that Erasmus Powe also built two other important houses in the town of Cheraw, both as wedding gifts for his daughters:

> The Hartzell House, which became Sherman's Headquarters in 1865.
>
> Enfield, which became headquarters for Sherman's second in command, Gen. Oliver Howard, during the Confederate War.

Erasmus Powe was a General during the time of the war of 1812.

After he died in 1817, his widow (Esther Ellerbe) lived there until her death in 1852, when it became the home of their son, Dr. Thomas Ellerbe Powe.

After the war, Capt. A.A. Pollock bought The Homestead. He and his family were living there when it accidentally burned on the afternoon of August 31, 1886, five hours before the great earthquake. It was a fine old house. Nothing remains but the beautiful avenue of cedars and elms.

Among Erasmus Powe's many descendants is North Carolina's well-known Senator Sam Ervin, Jr., who is descended from two of Erasmus's children!

To quote Sen. Sam Ervin in a letter to me in Philadelphia in 1976:

> *"I consider myself to be more of a Powe that the Powes themselves. I am a descendant of Erasmus Powe's son William Ellerbe Powe through my mother. James Robert Ervin was the son of Gen. Erasmus Powe's daughter, Elizabeth Powe, who married James Robert Ervin, of Cheraw, SC. I am a descendant of Elizabeth Powe through my father" (!)*

In a letter from Sam Ervin, Jr. to Mr. Edwin Guy, Camden, SC, March 15, 1942:

He listed the three grandsons of Gen. Erasmus Powe who were killed during the Confederate War:

> Thomas Erasmus Powe, killed at Gettysburg
> Hugh Torrence Powe, killed from wounds at Gettysburg James Robert Ervin, killed near Richmond, Virginia

III. DR. THOMAS ELLERBE POWE

(From All In One Southern Family, Volume 1 (AGM))

Thomas Ellerbe Powe, born on Feb. 21, 1800, was the son of General Erasmus Powe and Esther Ellerbe Powe. He graduated from the University of Pennsylvania Medical School in 1823, and came back to Cheraw to practice medicine. He married Charlotte Harrington, daughter of James Auld and Eleanor Wilson Harrington.

Dr. Powe was at one time one of the largest landowners in the Cheraw area and was quite a prominent citizen of the town, serving as commissioner of free schools and vestryman and warden of St. David's Episcopal Church. He was a member of the South Carolina House of Representatives in 1838, and a charter member and one-time president of the Pee Dee Medical Association. He is also credited with bringing the first tomatoes to South Carolina. At the time, they were called "love apples" and were thought to be poisonous.

He was a widower at the time of the Civil War (his wife having died on June 22, 1859) and was living at The Homestead during the visit of Sherman's troops. He wrote: "I, like everyone else, regard myself as dread fully used up by Mr. Sherman's army. It so happened that a Corps encamped on each of my plantations for 4 days. They burnt my mills, barns, gin houses and did not leave me a hoof of a cow or hog, and but one horse out of 40 (and that one my son-in-law Capt. McIver had in service). And not a feather or a fowl or anything else but a part of the clothes we had on. Everything went but the bare walls of my dwelling house. I rose one morning with 135 persons looking to me for supplies and had not a quart of corn or any ounce of meat. But the Almighty prepared a way for us to live, and we have lived. (This is quoted from Elsie Chapman Edmonds' book: John Chapman, Thomas Powe and Related Families.

Dr. Powe died on August 14, 1879, and he and his wife Charlotte Harrington Powe are buried in Old St. David's Cemetery.

I would like to mention here that when my sisters Es, Lou, and Pritch visited me in Philadelphia in 1978, we made a pilgrimage to the University of Pennsylvania Medical School and were successful in locating Thomas Ellerbe Powe's _Medical Dissertation. The Title: An Inaugural Dissertation on Amenorrhea. We had photographic copies_ made.

Fast forward to the year 2000 in Charleston, SC. My doorbell rang unexpectedly one day. There stood my niece Liz Bruno Eaton, here from her home in Mass., and holding a tremendous bunch of yellow daffodils. These, she explained, had been picked at her mother's home that morning in Cayce. It seems that years ago, my sisters Eleanor Bruno and Es Dargan had gone to Orange Hill, near Cheraw. And each of them dug up jonquil and daffodil bulbs that were growing wild at the site of Thomas Powe's home - built so long ago. These blossoms were from those daffodils of a long-ago family era - now speaking to us over all those years.

EARLY HISTORY -
FIRST SETTLEMENT

There was an article in *The Chronicle* about the Indians who
were living here "When White Man Came." - 1932

"When the first white settlers came up the Pee Dee River about 1730,
they found Indians - in fact, a small village which was situated just
north of Huckleberry Creek, at the top of the river hill. The Village
was probably located there as it was near the falls, where the fishing
was best. The falls are little more than shoals in the river, just above
the Seaboard trestle, a mile north of the town and known today as
Arrowhead Hill, where arrow heads can yet be picked up. Many of
these arrow heads are made of stone that is not found near here.
Some are of quartz, clear as crystal. These must have been brought
by Indians when they came to this locality.

"These Indians, which were the Cheraws, a detached part of the
Cherokee tribe, numbered possibly less than two hundred and had
not lived here more than 25 years when the white man came.

"The Indians had a graveyard here where the town was later
laid out. This small graveyard was between where the Baptist and
Methodist churches are now located, in the back part of the lot in
rear of the Misses McIver house, (Boxwood Hall).

"The writer *(Mr. Will Godfrey)* remembers his grandfather,
William Godfrey, telling him that when he was a boy in 1815, he
was afraid to go by this Indian graveyard, which had totem poles

in it, or poles with some colored objects tied on them, probably to keep evil spirits away.

"The Indians remained here, though gradually growing fewer in numbers, til about 1830 - or a century after the first white settlers arrived."